Matthew Donald.

Matthew Donald.

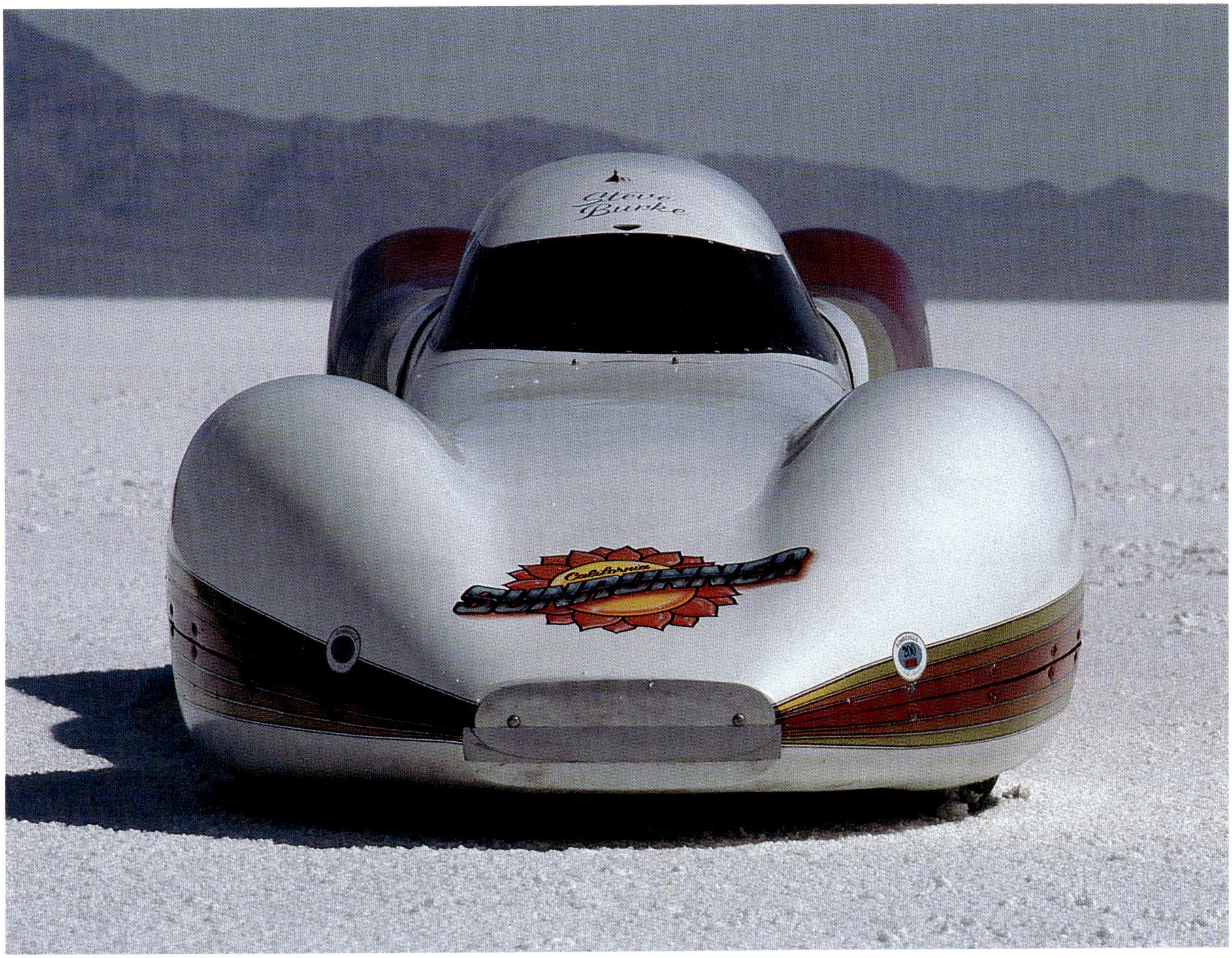
Steve Burke
California
SUNRUNNER

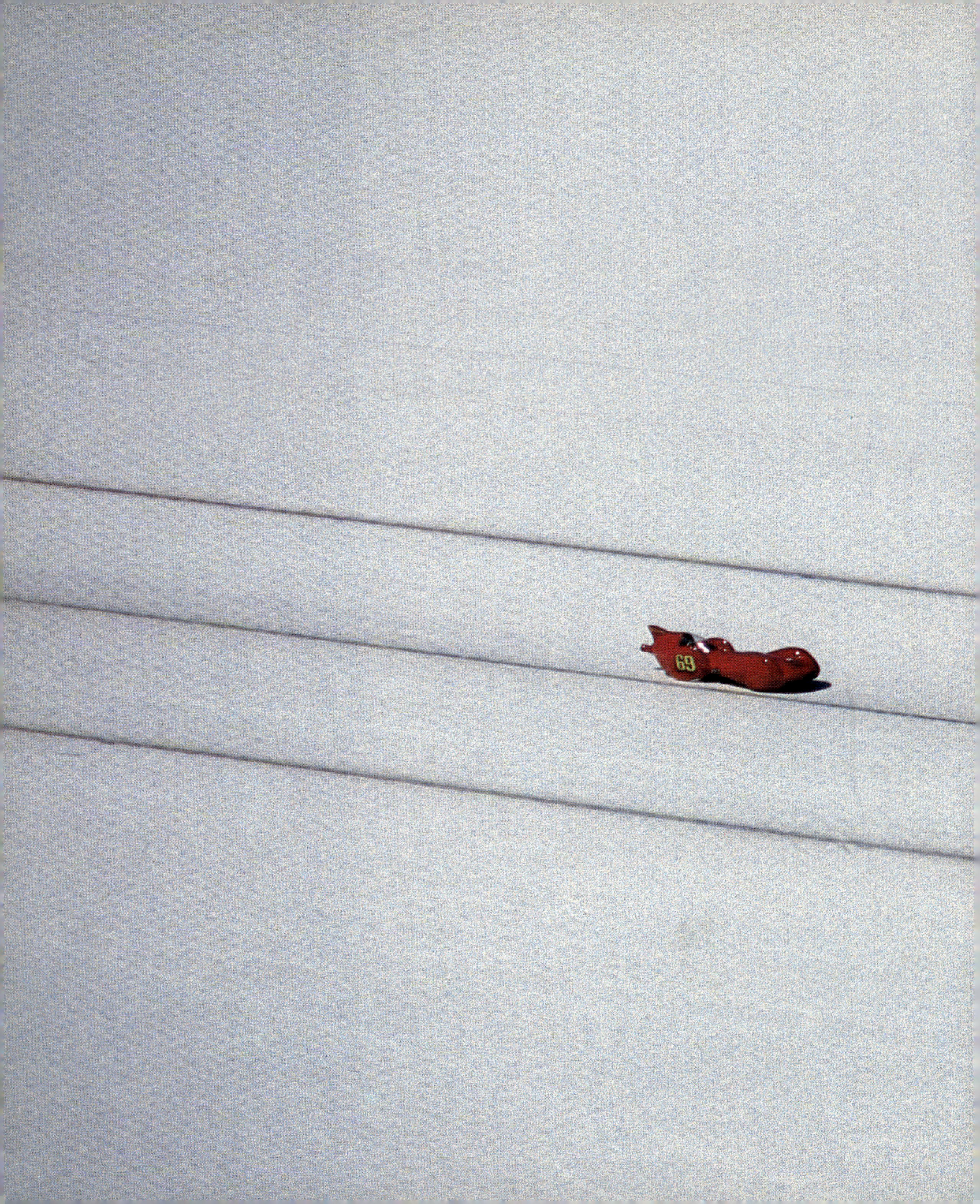
69

BONNEVILLE SALT FLATS

Speed limit 1,000 mph

George D. Lepp

Motorbooks International
Publishers & Wholesalers Inc
Osceola, Wisconsin 54020, USA

First published in 1988 by Motorbooks International Publishers & Wholesalers Inc, P O Box 2, 729 Prospect Avenue, Osceola, WI 54020 USA

© George D. Lepp, 1988

All rights reserved. With the exception of quoting brief passages for the purposes of review no part of this publication may be reproduced without prior written permission from the publisher

Motorbooks International is a certified trademark, registered with the United States Patent Office

Printed and bound in Hong Kong

The information in this book is true and complete to the best of our knowledge. All recommendations are made without any guarantee on the part of the author or publisher, who also disclaim any liability incurred in connection with the use of this data or specific details

We recognize that some words, model names and designations, for example, mentioned herein are the property of various automotive and component manufacturers. We use them for identification purposes only. This is not an official publication

Library of Congress Cataloging-in-Publication Data
```
Lepp, George D.
  Bonneville Salt Flats
  photography by George D. Lepp.
  ISBN 0-87938-306-2
  1. Bonneville Salt Flats Race, Utah. I. Title.
GV1033.5.B66L47 1988  796.7'2--dc19  88-11734 CIP
```

Motorbooks International books are also available at discounts in bulk quantity for industrial or sales-promotional use. For details write to Special Sales Manager at the Publisher's address

On the front cover: *Front view of Banks' 1988 Pontiac Trans Am with Don Stringfellow at the wheel. This is the world's fastest passenger car at an official speed of 268.003 mph. The Firebird has a stock body with numerous modifications underneath, including a 454 ci twin turbo, Pontiac big-block V-8 engine putting out over 1,600 hp. Pontiac's well-styled body gave the Banks crew a shape that has a drag coefficient of just under 0.30 and is stable at high speeds.*

On the back cover: *It's a lonely feeling with no one around at the end of the run. The hyperactivity of the starting line is replaced with miles of empty and silent salt. At the end of the run there's nothing for the driver to do while waiting for the chase crew to catch up, except pack up his or her braking chute. This is the modified sport number 30. It is an Opel sports car from the sixties with a 301 ci Chevrolet engine. Best speed for the Opel was a new record of 200.961 mph.*

On the frontispiece: *An example of radical streamlining. This Burke Bros. E/Fuel Streamliner first raced on the salt in 1985. The car was powered by a blown 258 ci small-block Chevy engine and was 25 feet long and only 54 inches wide at the front and 48 inches wide at the rear, with a height of 39 inches. The making of the distinctive body was unique in that a chassis was constructed and the basic body was formed around it using framing and wire mesh. Over that was blown a soft foam that allowed the final forming of the body shape. With the exact form ready, a fiberglass skin was formed over the foam with resin and cloth, the wire mesh removed, and another layer of fiberglass formed on the inside, making a strong and lightweight sandwich.*

At a recent Bonneville meet, the car lost a pin that secured one of the front wheels, causing the front end to dig in and veer to the side. Unfortunately the speed was over 270 mph, causing the streamliner to pencil-roll numerous times, destroying the car. Due to a sturdy roll cage, the driver, Steve Burke, walked away unhurt.

On the title page: *Number 69, the Red Head XX/Gas Streamliner at speed on the course, shown here from the air. The Ardun Mercury flathead-powered streamliner set a record of 212.040 mph.*

On this page: *With a speed limit of 1,000, the Bonneville racers have a long way to go before they get arrested for speeding. These street signs have been a part of the pits for many years.*

Contents

Introduction	6
The salt flats	9
Speed Week	21
Problems of going fast	54
Classes	70
Vehicles on the salt	98
Stopping	119
The 200 MPH Club	126

Introduction

For the past thirty-nine years, one week in late summer has been set aside by a group of racers to do one thing: go as fast as is humanly possible in motorized vehicles on the Bonneville Salt Flats. Only a few places exist where this endeavor is possible, or even tolerated. Here at Bonneville this behavior not only is tolerated, but has flourished to provide a safe facility for speed trial competition available to participants from all over the world.

There are no big money purses to win on the salt; just the satisfaction of being the best in a particular area of endeavor. The cost can be minimal or extreme, whatever it takes to accomplish the goal. Racing down the salt at ever-increasing speeds does have its dangers, and three drivers have lost their lives in pursuit of personal goals.

Several things are evident when one attends Speed Week. The first is the friendly camaraderie of the participants. Advice is exchanged, tools are loaned and lasting friendships are formed. Most of the participants have been here many times before, while newcomers are wholeheartedly welcomed.

The sights and sounds of Speed Week are exotic. If any hot rod blood runs in your veins, the feast to the eyes of colorful machinery set for ultimate speed is exciting. To later hear one of these vehicles start up, be pushed from the starting line and, with open exhausts and full throttle, expend its total energy as it disappears down the long black line, leaves a lasting impression.

The Bonneville Salt Flats are to a car what a smooth lake is to a speed boat. One can drive off in almost any direction for miles without limitations or obstructions. Sunset on the deserted salt, with only the car tracks to show anyone has ever been there, is quiet and peaceful.

The salt racers are a demanding group when it comes to the condition of the salt flat's surface. If not enough rain falls earlier in the year the salt dries up, leaving a cracked and rutted surface not fit to race on. If the rains come too close to the time of Speed Week, the salt flats become a vast shallow lake that is also unfit for racing. If everything is just right, the water level is just below the surface and a firm, flat track stretches out across the salt for at least seven miles.

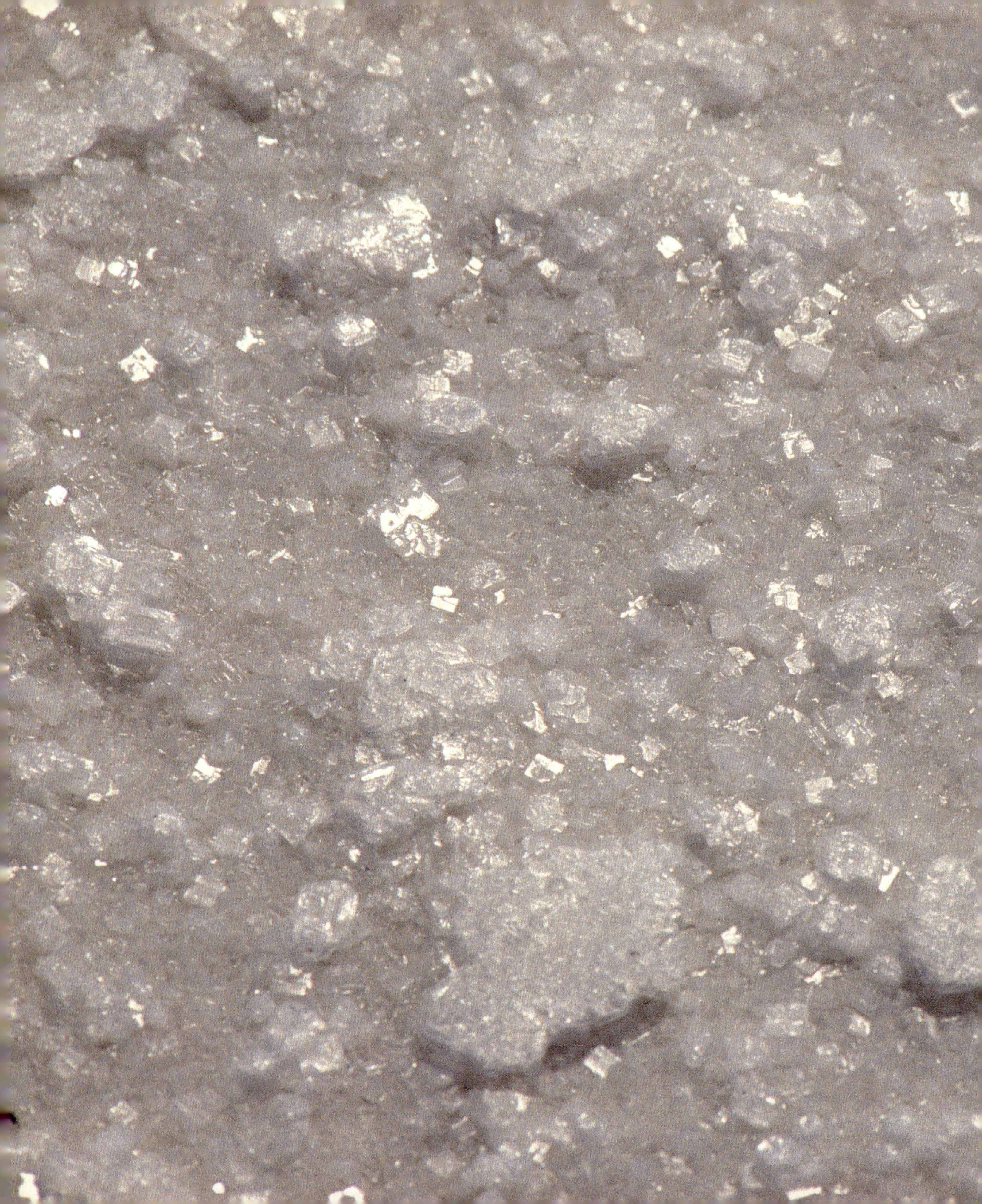

The salt flats

As one stands out on the Bonneville Salt Flats it would appear that the salt goes on forever and is infinitely deep. Appearances are deceiving. Even though the Great Salt Lake Desert, within which the salt flats are located, is huge (one hundred miles long by fifty miles wide), the pristine Bonneville salt area is only approximately fourteen miles long and six miles wide. Beneath the surface the salt is in layers, alternating with mud. The surface crust of salt is only about three inches thick.

Below the approximately one-foot-thick layers of salt and mud is a water table. In wet years and after recent rains the water table rises to the surface and forms a shallow lake. This shallow lake is moved back and forth over the salt flats by the wind until evaporation again resurfaces the flats with a smooth, flat layer of the remaining salt residue.

Stretching across the surface of the pristine section of the Bonneville salt lies the track: eighty feet wide and seven miles long with black lines down each side and the center. The course is laid out each year with accurate surveying equipment so that all distances are within inches of being perfect. At each mile is a large, yellow, numbered marker to let the drivers know their location as they speed down the otherwise featureless track. Some drivers even experience so much vibration that they can't read the mile numbers and must count the markers as each speeds by in a blur.

There is an approach of two miles from the starting line to gain speed before the first timing trap. The first quarter of the third mile is used in

A closer look at the surface of the salt flats shows a crystalline structure. Beneath the three- to four-inch salt surface are alternating layers of salt and mud. The separate layers affirm earlier times when mud washed down from the surrounding mountains and covered the salt flats. The salt returned during times of surplus water that allowed the salt to percolate to the surface. Fortunately, the present cycle favors the formation of an excellent salt base. Along the edges of the salt flats and near the drainage ditches the surface salt crust is thin with underlying water. Numerous visitors to the salts have not heeded warning signs and broken through the surface into the corrosive brine.

qualifying times only, followed by timing traps at the end of the third, fourth and fifth miles.

Ideally, the track would be better if it were longer so that the heavier cars could have more distance to accelerate and also have more room to stop at the end of a fast run. Depending on the timing of the rain in a given year the track can be extended when the salt at the end of the track has had a chance to dry out.

In years past, the salt area used for Speed Week was also set up with a large oval track ten miles in length. Endurance races of a few hours to weeks were held with sustained speeds of over 200 mph. All remains of this track have long since been erased by the salt.

Previous page
Sunrise over a section of the salt flats that was covered with water from thunderstorms gives us a good idea of how this area looked eons ago when the salt flats and the Great Basin were all under water. The group of mountains in the distance is called Floating Mountain.

An overview of the racetrack during Speed Week showing the start line and the track stretching seven miles into the distance. Spectators line up in a V at the start and along the two roads that parallel the track out to about a quarter mile. The drivers leave a bustling start line to streak down an empty track with only three black lines and the spaced mile markers to guide the way. If trouble develops along the path, drivers are instructed to pull to the left of the track; if all goes well and no emergency exists, the exit for each vehicle is to the right. Spotters with radios are positioned at each mile marker to monitor the progress of the vehicles on the track.

A summer thunderstorm threatens the qualifying with an occasional cloud burst. It takes but one cloud burst to cover the track with a layer of water that may take days to evaporate.

In 1982 everyone showed up to race, but the salt was covered with a layer of water and the dejected racers headed back home without a single run down the salt. In 1983, Speed Week was canceled before anyone even arrived, due to the flooded salt flats.

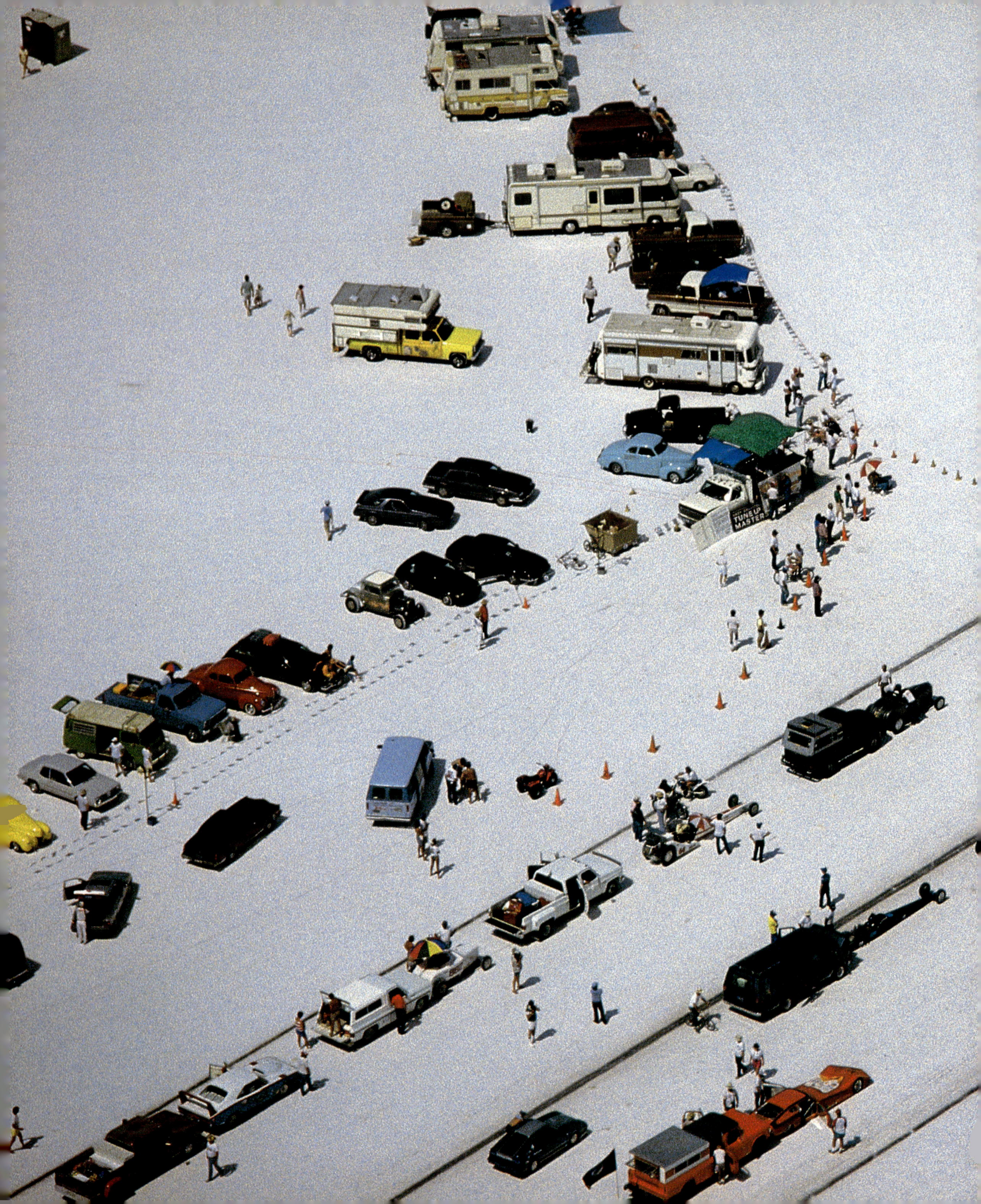
TUNE UP MASTERS

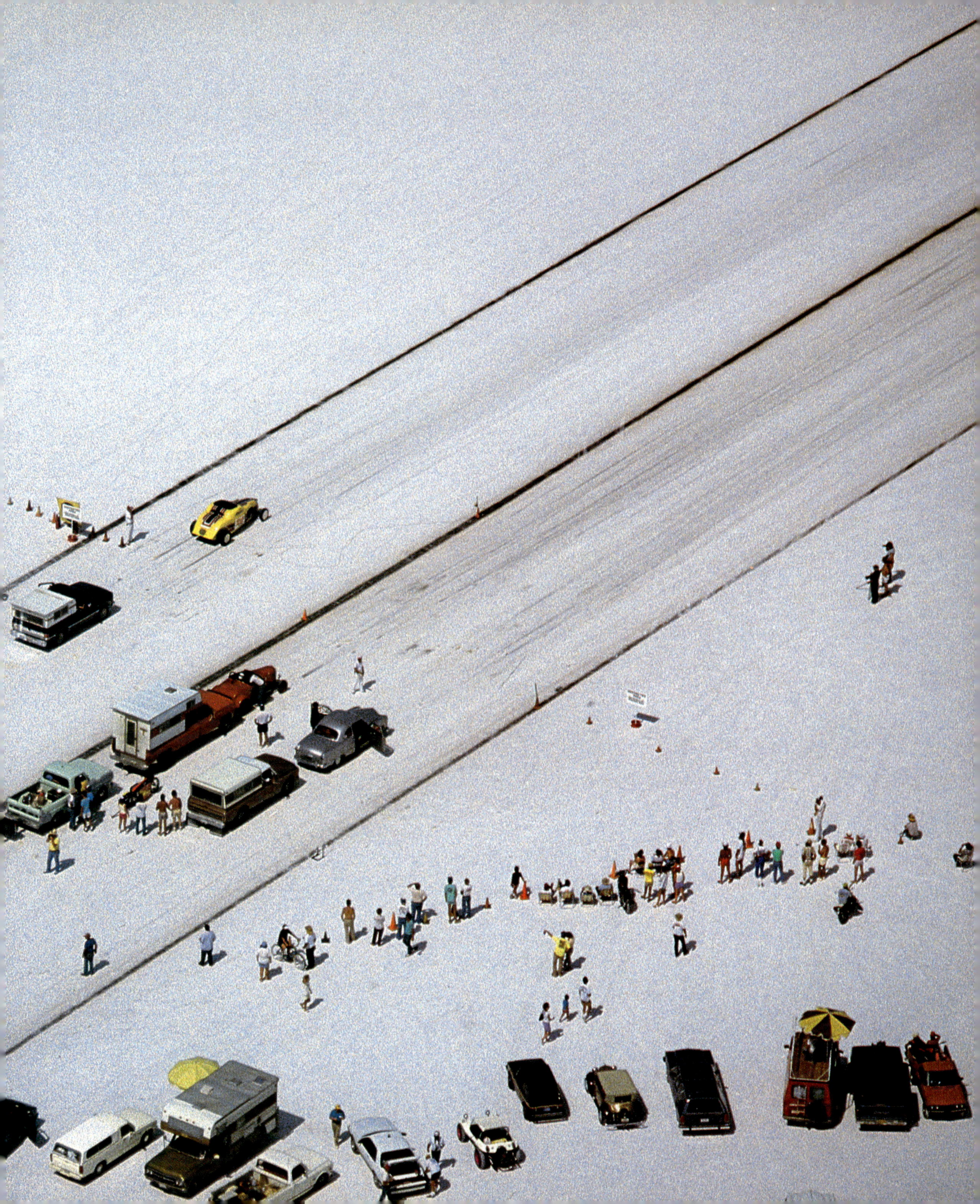

Previous page
An aerial view of the starting line shows the racers and their support vehicles waiting to make their qualifying runs during the afternoon. Even though the racers may start on the left or right of the center line, each driver has his or her own idea as to which part of the course will give the best traction. Those that surpass the existing record by at least 0.001 mph will be allowed to make a two-way record run attempt the next morning.

Elmo Gillette places the five-mile marker into the holes drilled in the salt. He and his crew use the most sophisticated surveying equipment to ensure the accuracy of the distance markers. Several possible course layouts are considered each year, with the final one decided on by the Bureau of Land Management. The main consideration is the condition of the salt in order to give the longest track length. Some years the track can be as long as nine miles, giving a longer run before the timed miles. Usually the total length of the track is seven miles.

From the starting line the driver chooses the line in the track that he's going to follow. Yellow mile markers come up at mile one and mile two. At the start of mile two a quarter-mile timing trap is located for qualifying purposes only. At the beginning of mile three another light is located to give the speed for the first timed mile. Timing lights are also located at the beginning of the fourth and fifth miles, giving a total of four recorded speeds: the first quarter, first full mile, second mile and third mile. Once the driver sees the five-mile marker it's time to shut it down and bring the vehicle to a stop. Two more miles are allotted to this endeavor.

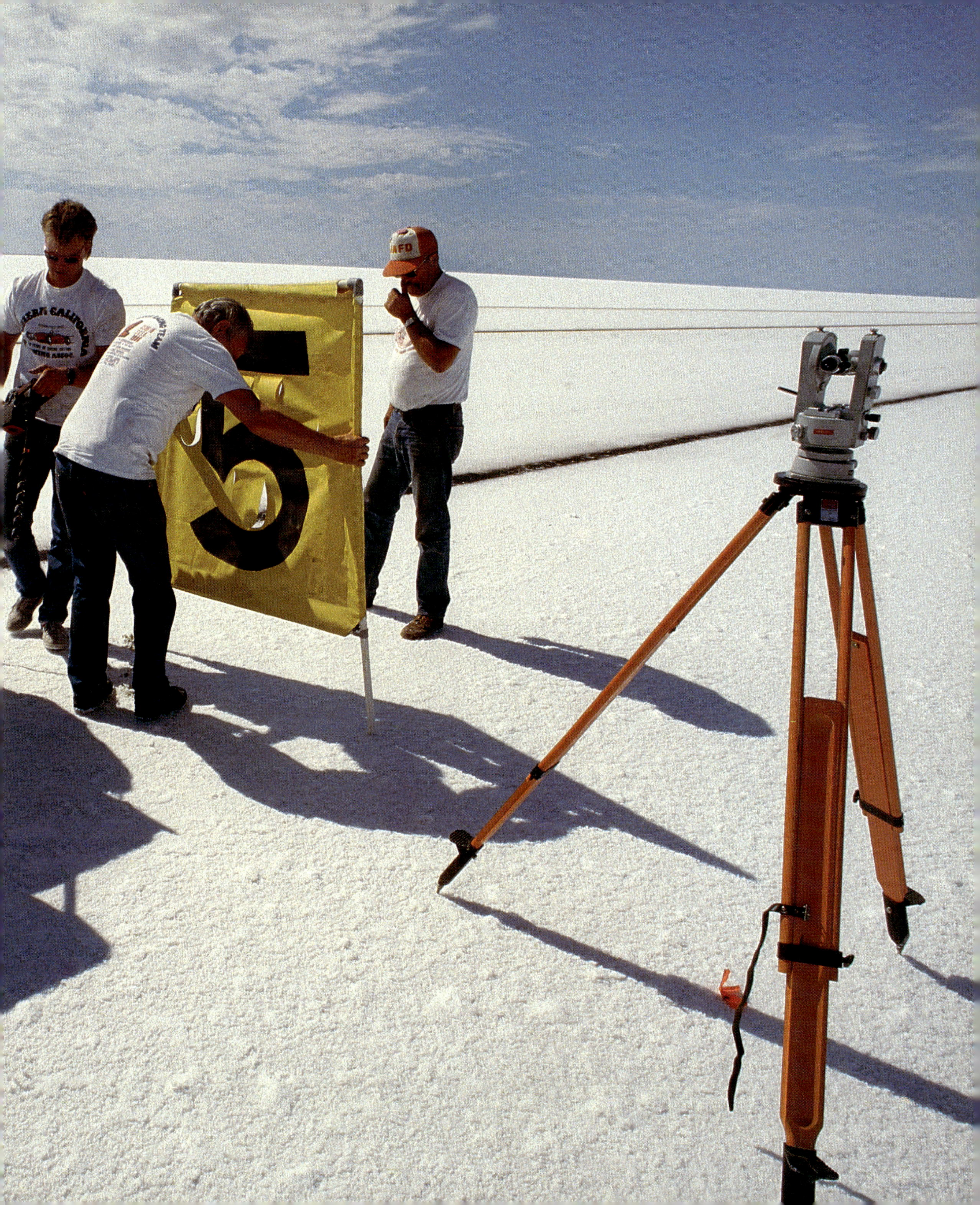
5

Backup timing equipment under the regular timing tower. These state-of-the-art electronics check the accuracy of the regular timing equipment and are being tested before the implementation the following year. Each vehicle's time is printed out by the computer and radioed to the announcing stand at the starting line. The drivers don't know if they've qualified or set a new record until their support crews catch up with them at the end of the track.

John Helash, the 1987 president of the sponsoring Southern California Timing Association, addresses the drivers. The drivers' meeting informs them of any new course and safety information and rule changes, and allows the drivers to ask questions or air any concerns about the meet.

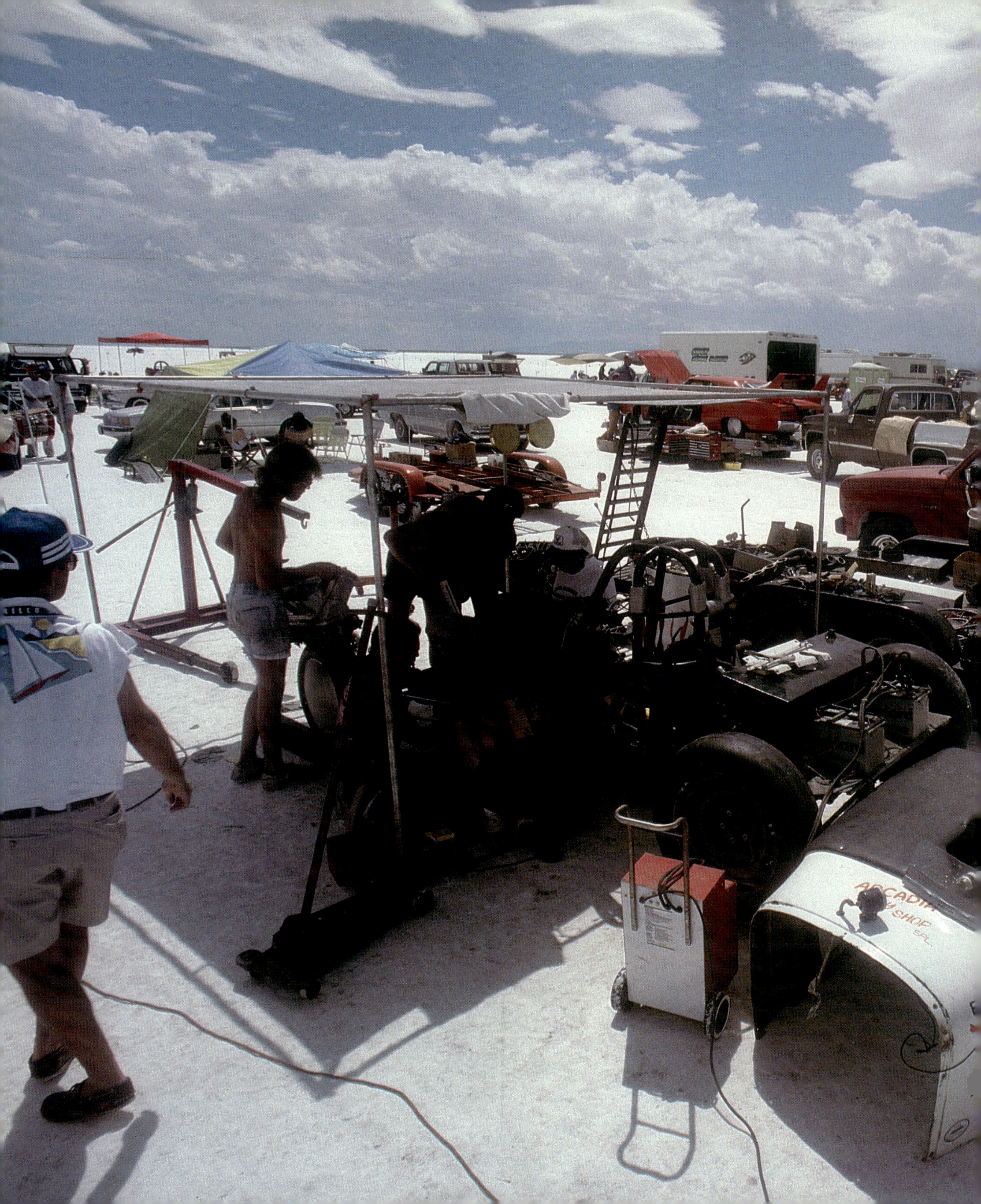
SHOP
SPL.

Speed Week

Safety inspection

By Saturday most of the participants have arrived in the Wendover, Nevada, area and begin preparation for a week of racing. The first item on the week's agenda is Saturday's safety inspection held at the Wendover airport. The race vehicles line up and are scrutinized by the Bonneville National Officials for compliance with the rules for driver safety. Volunteers, headed by the sanctioning Southern California Timing Association (SCTA), comprise these officials and also administer all aspects of Speed Week. No vehicle is allowed to run for qualification until it has satisfactorily passed all safety requirements.

Safety requirements on the salt flats include the use of certified drivers' helmets, fire suits with gloves and boots, roll bar and roll cage structures in the vehicles, competition seats and seatbelts, special tires rated for the projected speed of the vehicle, at least one parachute for vehicles that qualify at over 175 mph, and a fire extinguisher discharge system. For the drivers' and participants' safety, several ambulance crews are stationed along the course and manned by special medical personnel. Either airplane or helicopter evacuation is available in case of severe injury.

Qualifying

Sunday's schedule starts early with a drivers' meeting to clarify rules and procedures. After all is said, the first of over 200 entered vehicles are ready to make their runs down the salt in an attempt to qualify for the next morning's record runs.

New cars and new drivers may be required to make a pass down the course at less than full throttle, and all drivers must have a current SCTA

Clutches, manifolds, tools and parts everywhere as the Paul Winson team works in the pits to ready a massive 605 ci Pontiac engine. The monster engine resides in the number 482 A/Street Roadster. The car later turned a speed of 209.616 mph to set a new record for its class. Crews are often required to completely tear down an engine overnight to replace a part or try a new idea that may give them the added power needed for a couple extra miles per hour.

competition license. A category E license is the slowest, for vehicles of 124 mph or less; a category A license is the fastest, for vehicles that are capable of 200 mph or faster. The driver must make a pass at the speed for each category to qualify for that license.

How does one qualify for a speed record run? If a vehicle is capable of over 175 mph, the first run needs to be over that speed to qualify for the long track. The short track consists of only the timing traps at the end of the first quarter of the third mile and the end of the full three miles. The long track adds the traps at the end of four miles and the end of five miles. During the qualifying runs a vehicle must surpass the existing class record by 0.001 mph to participate in the next morning's record runs.

For those classes that do not have an established speed record, a rules committee sets a minimum speed based on experience, other classes, engines to be used and body styles.

Record runs

Each morning after a day of qualifying, those vehicles that have surpassed existing records by at least 0.001 mph line up at 8 a.m. for an attempt to break the existing speed record. All vehicles complete the first direction of the two-way run, and the drivers have approximately one hour to prepare their vehicles for the return run.

The average of the two runs is considered for the record. The times of the two runs must also be from the same clocked mile. If the best time on the first run was in the fifth mile, then the return run time in the fifth mile would be the time used for the average toward the record.

Inspection of record breakers

Any vehicle breaking a record proceeds directly to an impound/inspection area to confirm compliance with body class, engine displacement and safety requirements. The appointed officials can require the vehicle owner to tear down any component for inspection. A direct measurement of displacement can be taken by either removing the head or dropping the oil pan, whichever is best to measure the diameter of the cylinder and the length of the stroke. With motorcycles, a cylinder is chosen and a measured amount of oil is placed into the cylinder opening.

Happenings

It's not all race and no play as the drivers and crews enjoy the food and gaming establishments at Wendover. Happenings on the salt also break up the continued runs of cars and bikes down the course. A few years ago a military jeep drove up to the announcer's stand and had the whole track cleared for the possibility of an emergency landing by a B-1 bomber that was in trouble overhead. Fortunately the seven-mile-long landing strip wasn't needed, as the plane made its way back safely to Edwards Air Force Base.

Another plane interruption occurred when a magazine publisher landed his private P80 jet on the track during qualifying. A great landing strip, but a little hairy for those on the course.

The great expanse of white, featureless salt tends to disorient passing birds; and a favorite pastime for the racers is to see who can catch the most helpless birds, place them in paper bags and take them back to Wendover for release. The exhausted birds seek the cover of the shade under vehicles, making the catching not too difficult.

The week's proceedings may be halted due to many different reasons. Salt corrodes wires for communication and timing. Errant race cars sever wires or knock out timing lights. On one occasion, a wayward mouse curled up in the shade of a timing light cover blocking its function; it was dispatched and the qualifying continued.

Some blue outdoor carpeting helps the Mazda RX-7 team keep the salt out of critical parts as they prepare the car for qualification. The only way to gain access to the underworkings of the low sports coupe is to tilt it up on one side. The Mazda RX-7 is the culmination of a two-year project headed by Racing Beat of Southern California. They took a 1986 Mazda RX-7 body, put a racing suspension under it, tweaked the turbo, two-rotor, 80 ci Wankel engine to a phenomenal 530 hp, and blew out the class record by over 37 mph.

mazda
RX 7
ROTARY ROCKET
GOODYEAR
ENKEI
Racing Beat
ROTARY PERFORMANCE PRODUCTS
Anaheim, Cal.
ULTRA
IGNITION SYSTEMS
NGK
CAR AND DRIVER

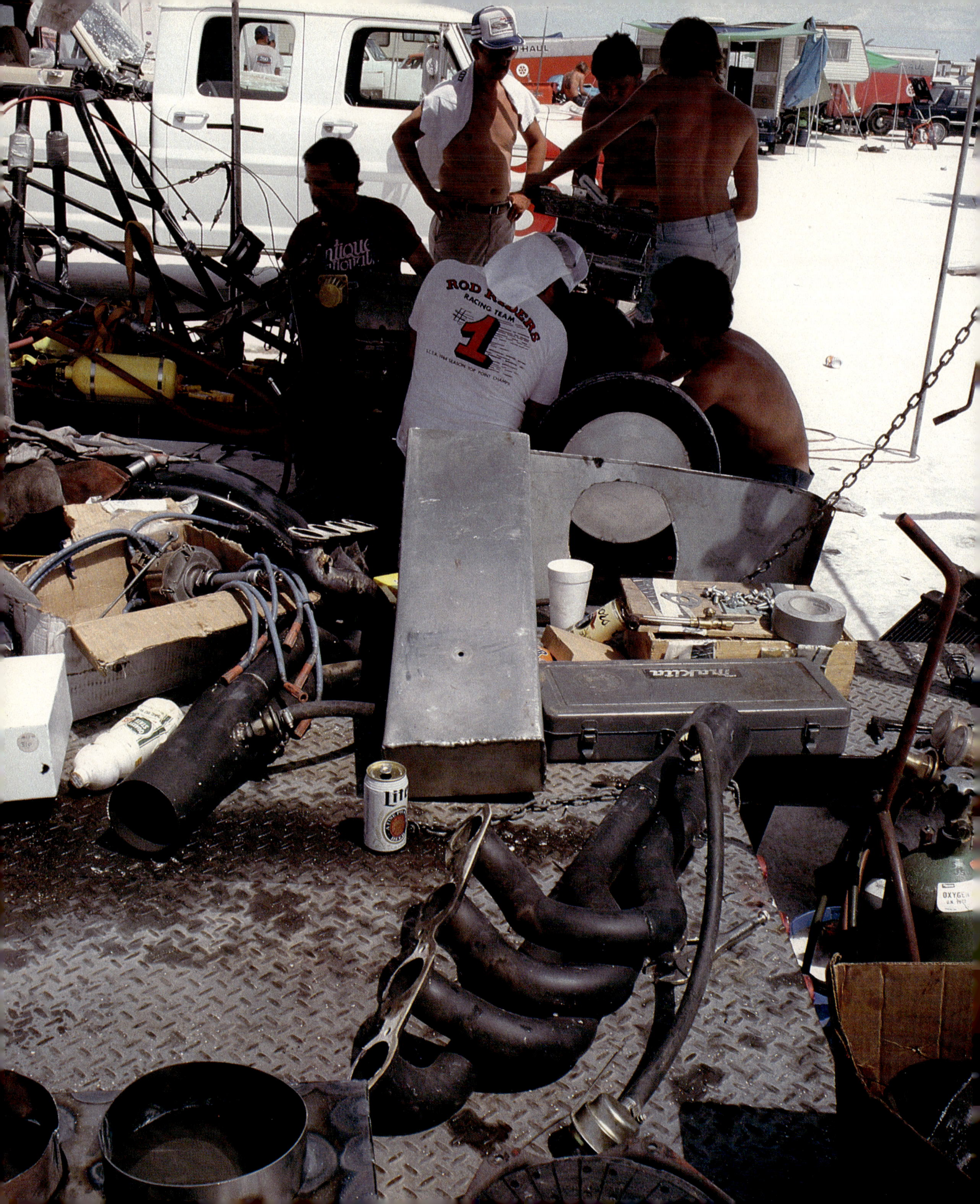
RACING TEAM
1
Lite
OXYGEN

The pit area around the Paul Winson street roadster looks like an auto parts warehouse with a clutch, headers and miscellaneous engine parts littering the area. The complete teardown of an engine is a common sight during Speed Week.

Take a Ferrari 308 GTB chassis, slick GTO body panels, drop in a Chevy five-liter V-8 that cranks out a claimed 600 hp, and you've got a beautiful D/Modified Sports car that ran at a speed of just over 192 mph.

During the Saturday before the start of racing, inspectors carefully check out each vehicle for compliance with the safety and class rules. Each entrant is responsible for determining which class he or she wishes to run in and then for complying with that class' specifications. The inspectors are volunteers from the Southern California Timing Association. Many of these inspectors have raced at Bonneville in years past and all have been certified through a training program.

Inspectors pour a measured amount of oil into one of the cylinders of a record-breaking motorcycle to verify its displacement. All record breakers are subject to verification of class rules before a record becomes official. This may very well entail the tearing down of an engine so a direct measurement of the displacement can be verified. The 1300 cc bike being tested here set a record of 212+ mph.

During the two-way record runs the far end of the course becomes the location of a makeshift pit as the driver and mechanics of an F/Fuel Roadster get ready to make the return run for the record. The cars and motorcycles usually only have one hour before they must make the return run. Any work can be done to the engine; in fact, one crew tore down an engine to replace a burned piston in an hour and a half. Those that can't return are disqualified, even if the speed of the first run was over the record. Before another record attempt can be made, the vehicle must again qualify at 0.001 mph over the existing record during the regular afternoon qualifying runs.

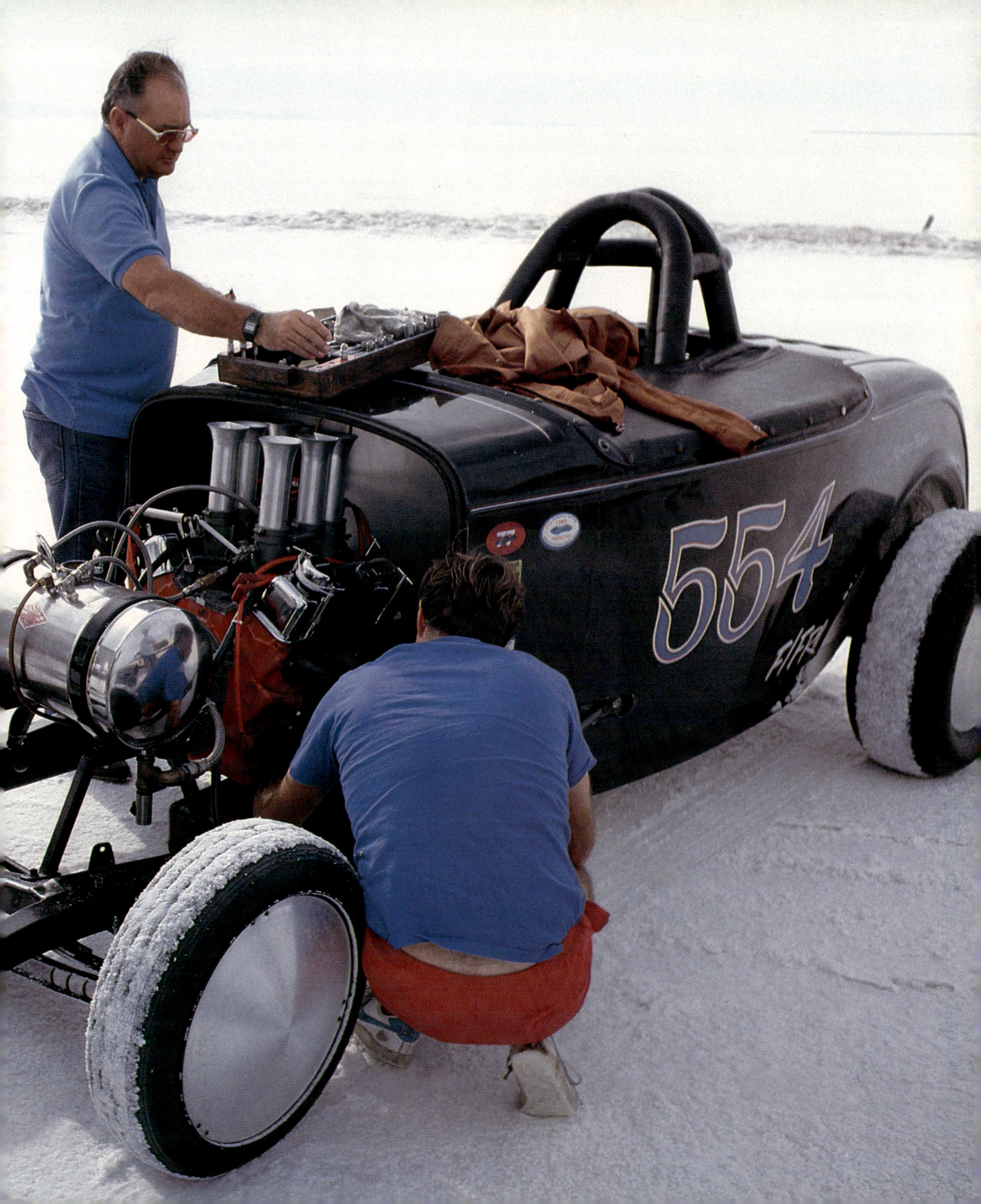
554

Bill Lattin gets buttoned into the custom aluminum-bodied Red Head streamliner prior to his record run. The engine in this vehicle is a 1949 Ford/Mercury flathead with special Ardun heads producing 300 hp from the 274 ci. The old flathead turned 212.040 mph without the benefit of a blower and using pump gasoline. This car first competed at the salt in 1962 and still looks sleek and current. Note the need for the removable steering wheel to get the driver into the tight cockpit.

One method to increase power from a turbocharged engine is to run the intake air through an intercooler to supercool it prior to its being injected with fuel into the engine cylinders. Crew members place 250 pounds of crushed ice into the 95-gallon intercooler of the Gale Banks Pontiac Trans Am. The intercooled engine puts out 1,600 hp from 454 ci, thanks to the twin turbos and intercooler.

31

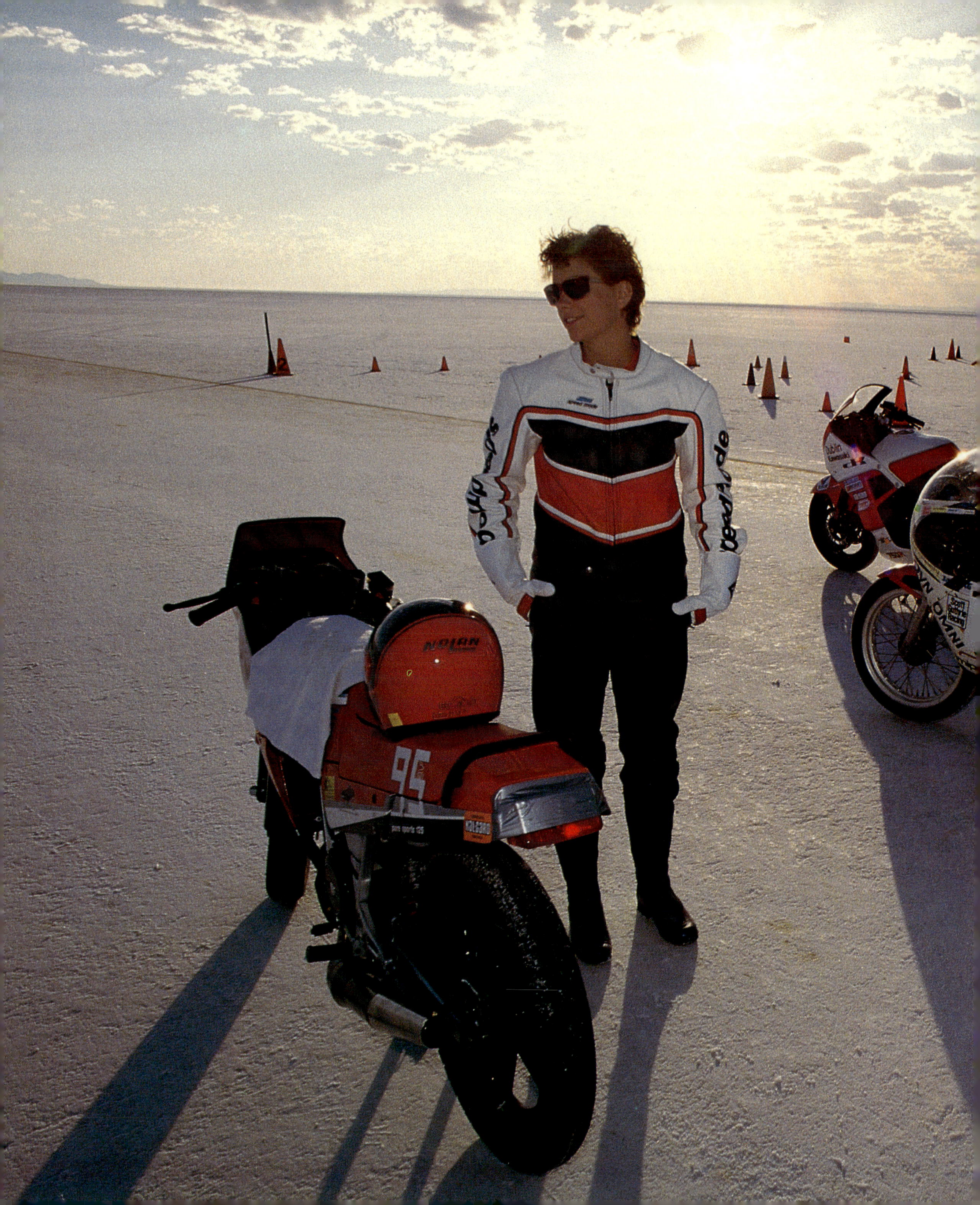
NOLAN
95

Getting ready for the morning record attempts. Belen Wagner stands next to her 125 cc Italian Fantic-powered bike. She later set a record for her class at 90.522 mph. The slowest record at Speed Week is 62.134 mph for the 50 cc motorcycles, while the fastest record is in the A/Fuel Streamliners at 354.330 mph.

33

Doc Jeffries displays the numerous Speed Week patches that attest to his years on the salt. During the seven days when it was possible to set records in both 1986 and 1987, Doc and his Ford–Mercury EXP/LN7 set a new record each of those days. In just three years he has set nine records that still stand.

One car can set numerous records by having its body panels or engine changed, using a different type of fuel or switching to a quick-change rear end. By simply changing body panels a four-passenger Ford EXP can be changed into a two-passenger Mercury EXP and run for a different record.

A Mooneyman blower gets bolted onto a huge 510 ci Chevrolet engine residing in the number 333 AA/Gas Roadster of Varni, Walsh, Walsh and Cusak. The Mooneyman is similar to the General Motors blowers used on highway diesel trucks. Note the lack of brakes on the front of this 220+ mph roadster.

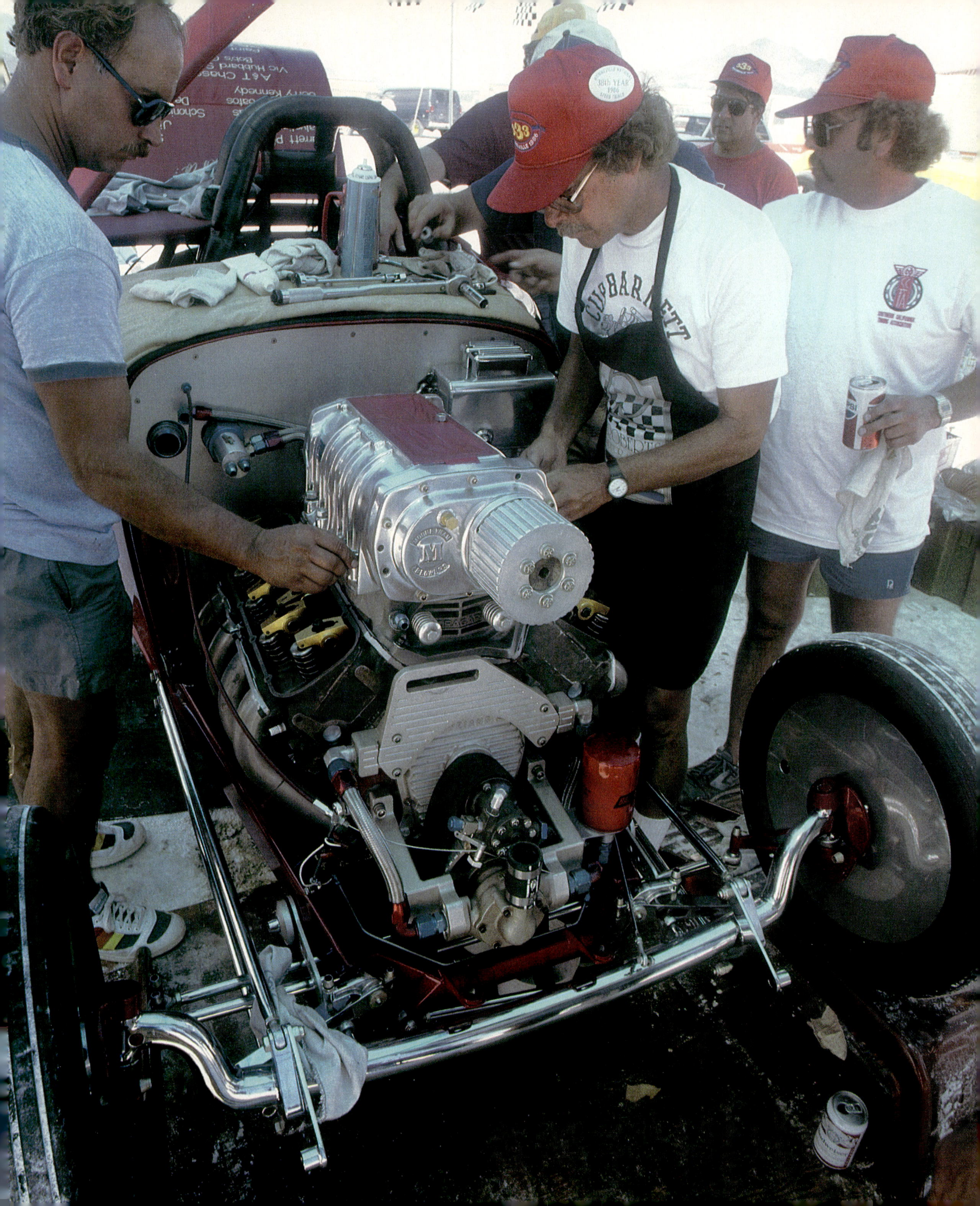
38th YEAR
1986

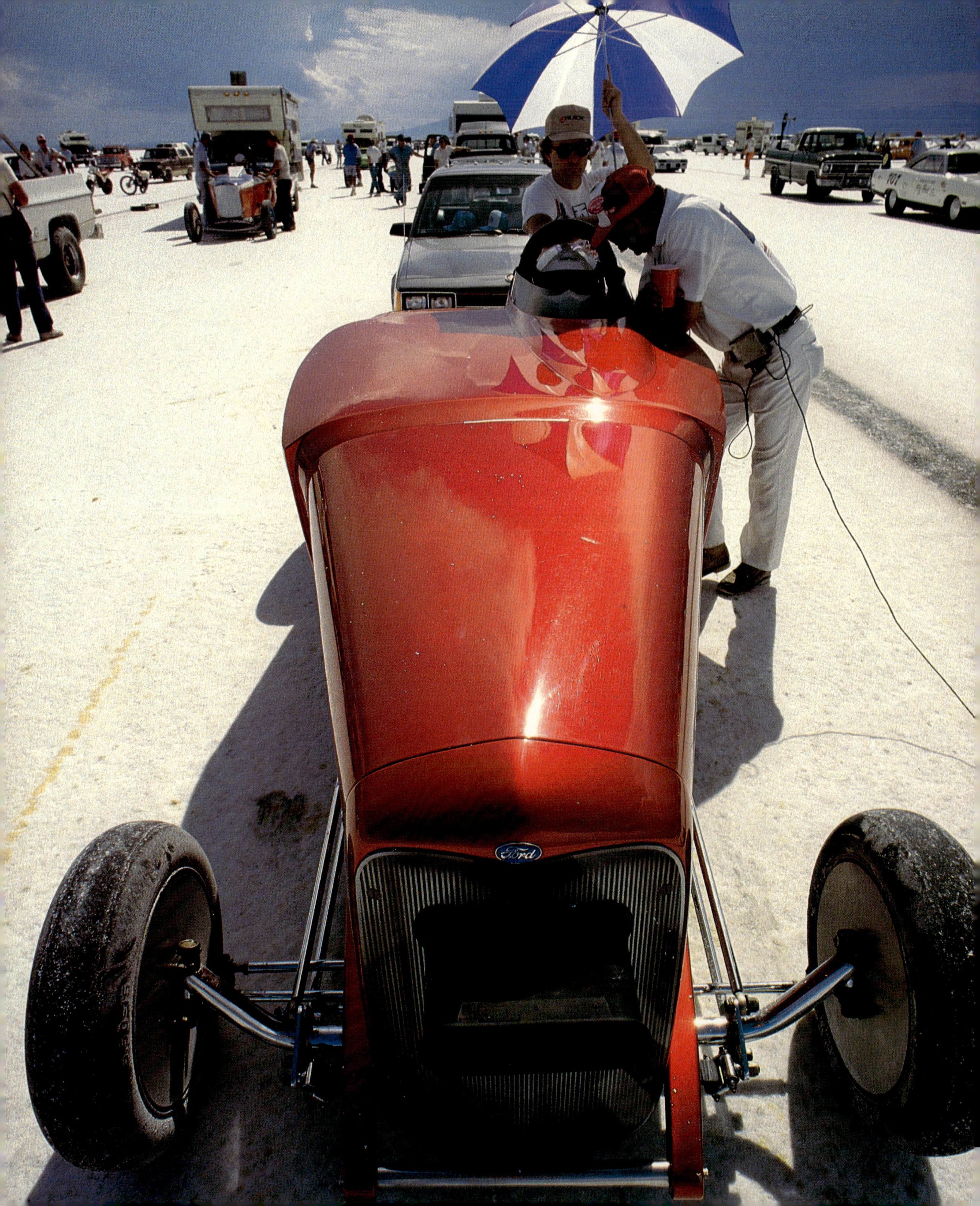
Ford

A gas roadster with a 371 ci Chevrolet gets ready to head down the salt. The umbrellas were used to keep drivers cool from the sun and later keep them dry from the thunderstorm approaching in the background.

The drivers wait at the starting line in their own sweat and go over the upcoming run in their minds. Even a few minutes in a complete Nomex fire suit can bake a driver from the inside out.

37

Scott Guthrie hangs his hat on the salt. Coming to the salt each year from Florida, Scott holds more motorcycle records than any other rider. By bringing more than one motorcycle and several engines, Scott has been able to set at least one record every day of Speed Week from 1983 through 1987. The top speed record for motorcycles that are only partially streamlined is just over 230 mph, turned in by Dave Campos on a Harley in 1974. The absolute speed for a motorcycle, this one being streamlined, during Speed Week is 318.598 mph by Don Vesco of Laguna Hills, California, in 1978.

Drivers gather at the start line for a briefing prior to the start of Sunday's qualifying runs.

This is no kid's tricycle. The three-wheeler, belonging to Clupper Racing, is powered by a 2000 cc engine. It turned a record speed of 175.786 mph—one of the faster tricycles on the block. The three-wheeled cycles have the advantage of two wheels driving power to the salt, but can be unstable at speed if not driven properly.

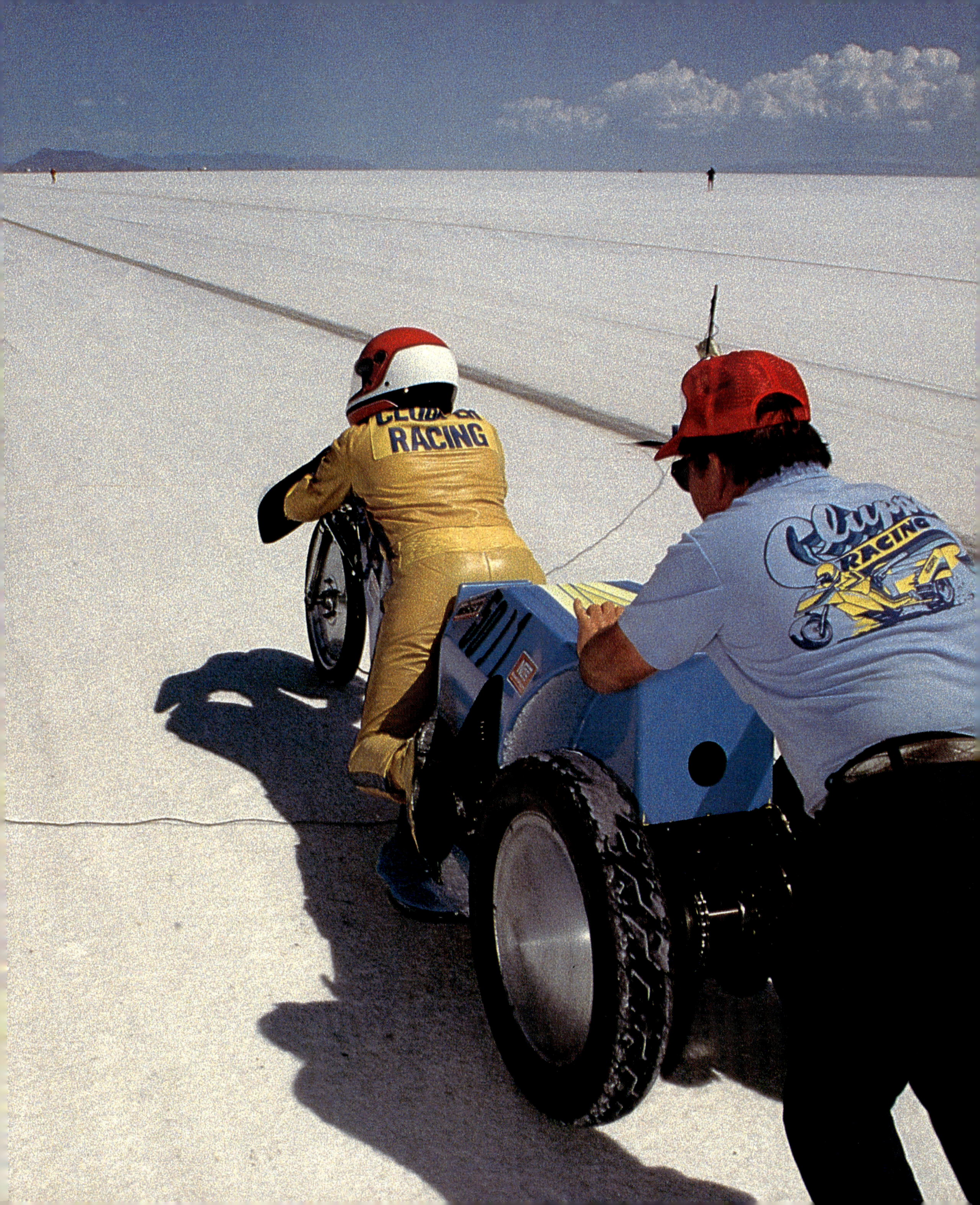
RACING
RACING

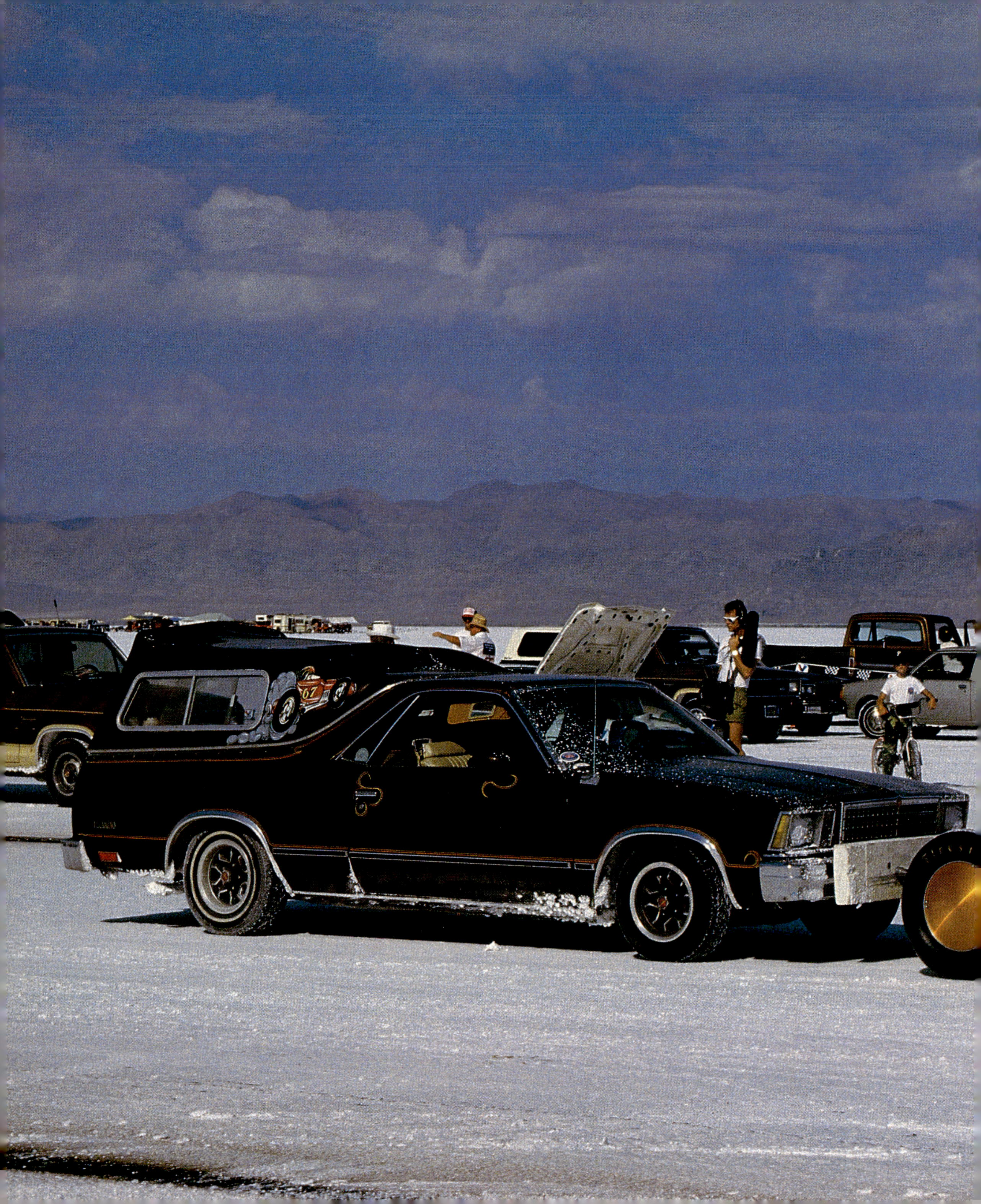

ANDY GRANATELLI'S
TUNE UP
MASTERS
MUST HAVE
PIT PASS
TO ENTER
THIS AREA
Best Buy Gaskets
67
MGM
HALIBRAND
Bob Butler

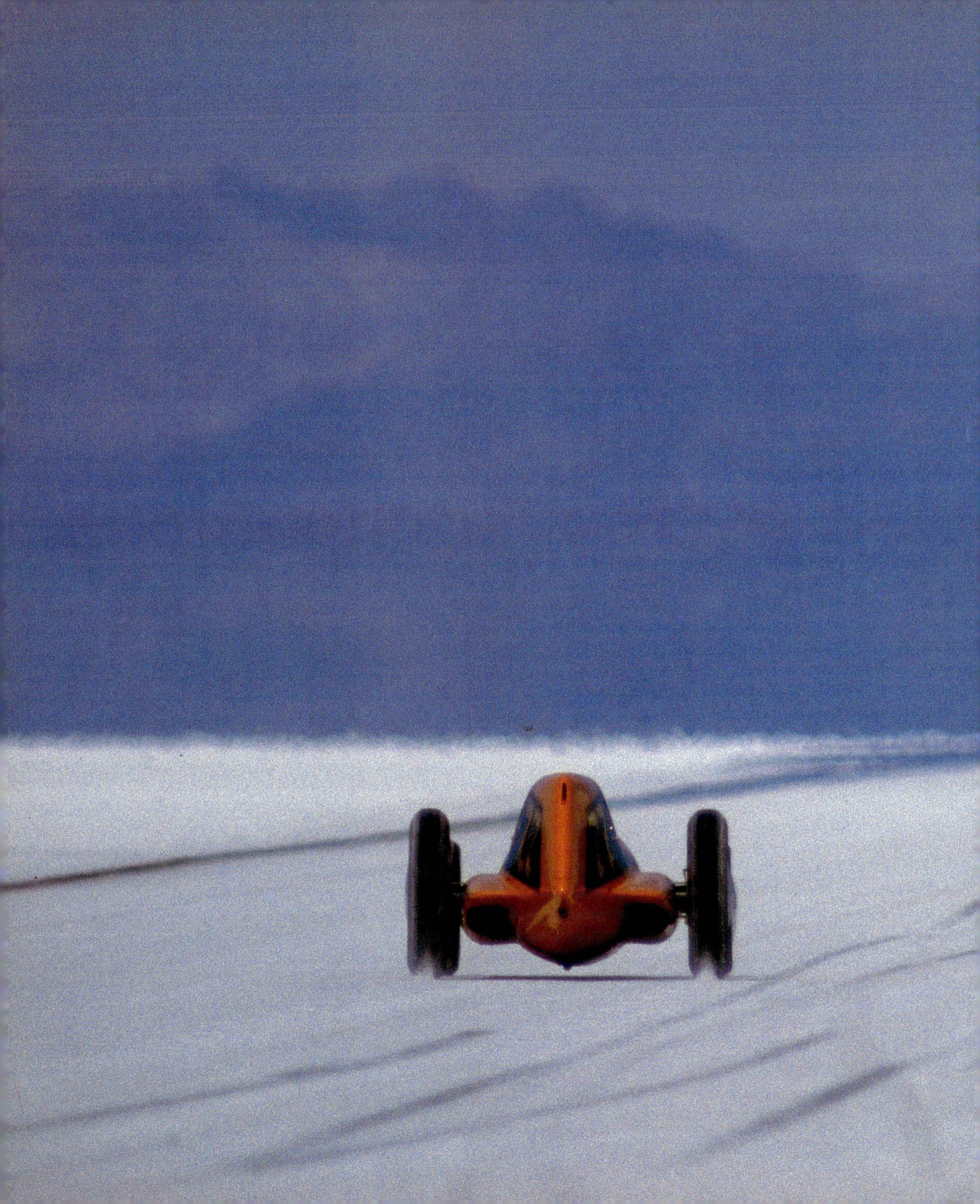

Previous page
Number 67, a B/Fuel Modified Roadster gets ready to thunder down the track with a 454 ci Chevrolet engine. The vehicle behind is a push car to get the roadster up to a speed where the engine will start.

No Nitro Hammond heads down the track with mile markers in the distance. The B/Gas Streamliner set a record of 251.750 mph. At that speed the markers fly past the driver very quickly. With three lines marking the course, all the driver needs to do is keep the car between two of them.

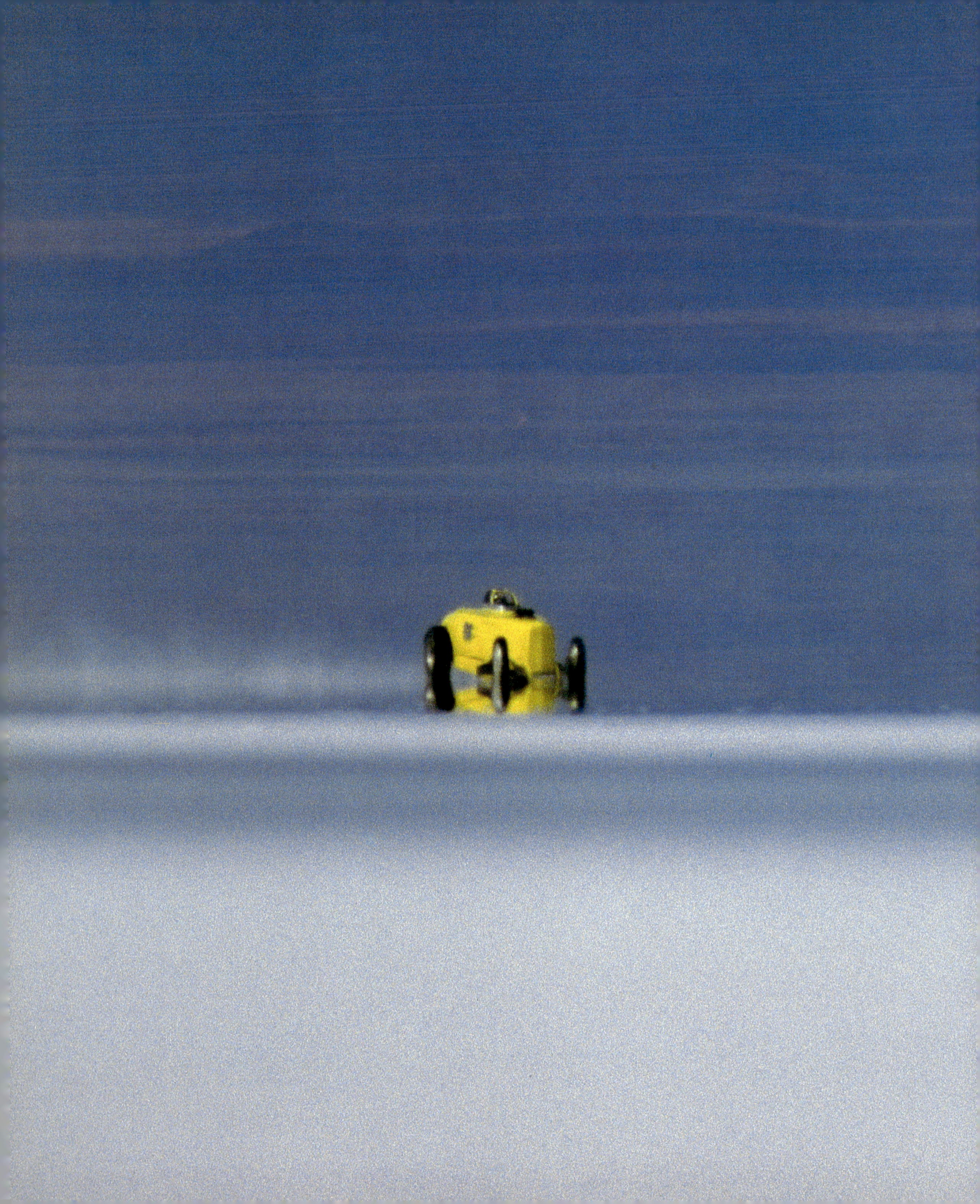

A distant roadster approaches through the mirage. The thunder of the "highboy" roadster could be heard for miles before they appeared out of the shimmering heat waves. The faster cars also set up a roostertail of salt behind them.

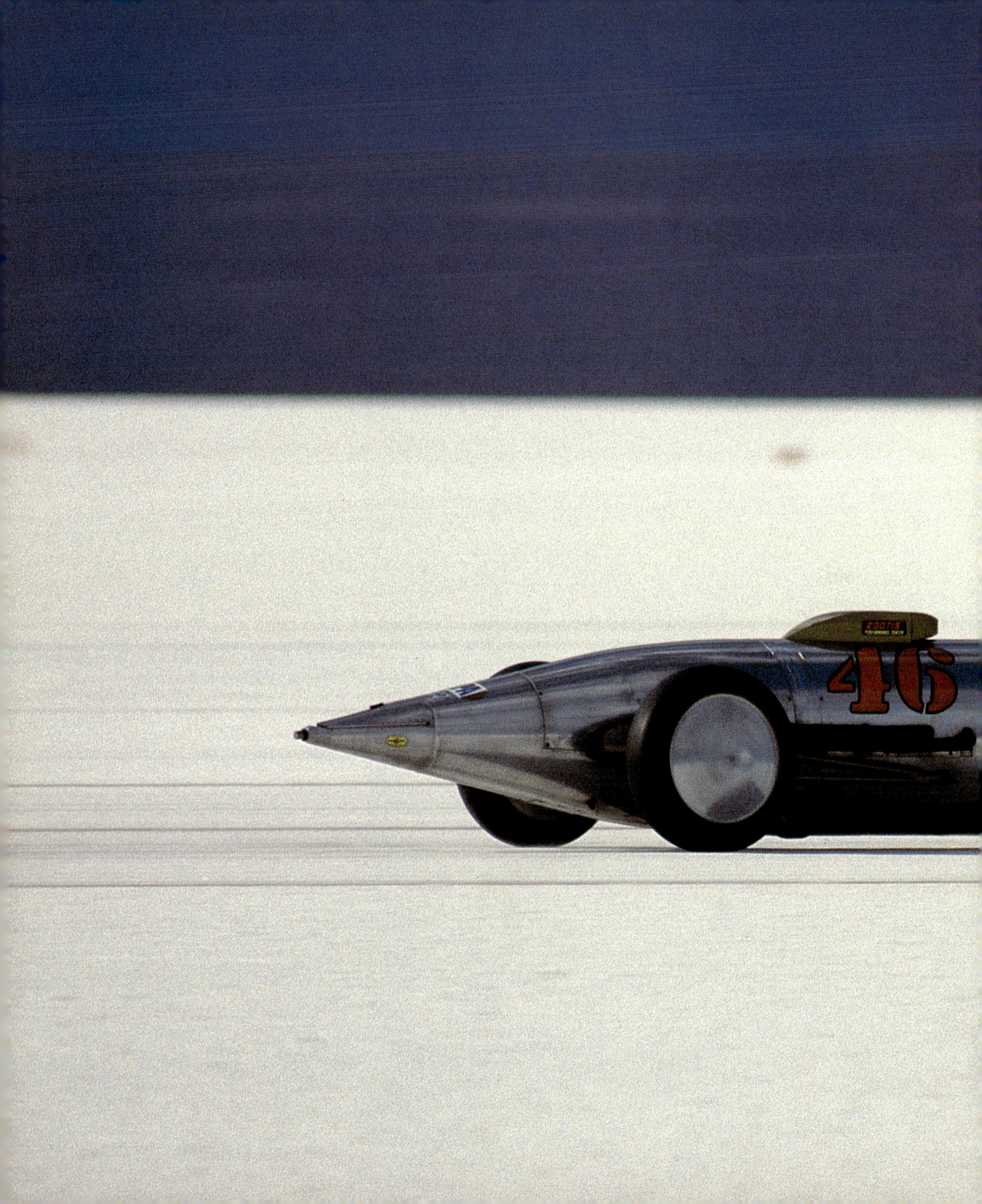
ZOOTIS
46

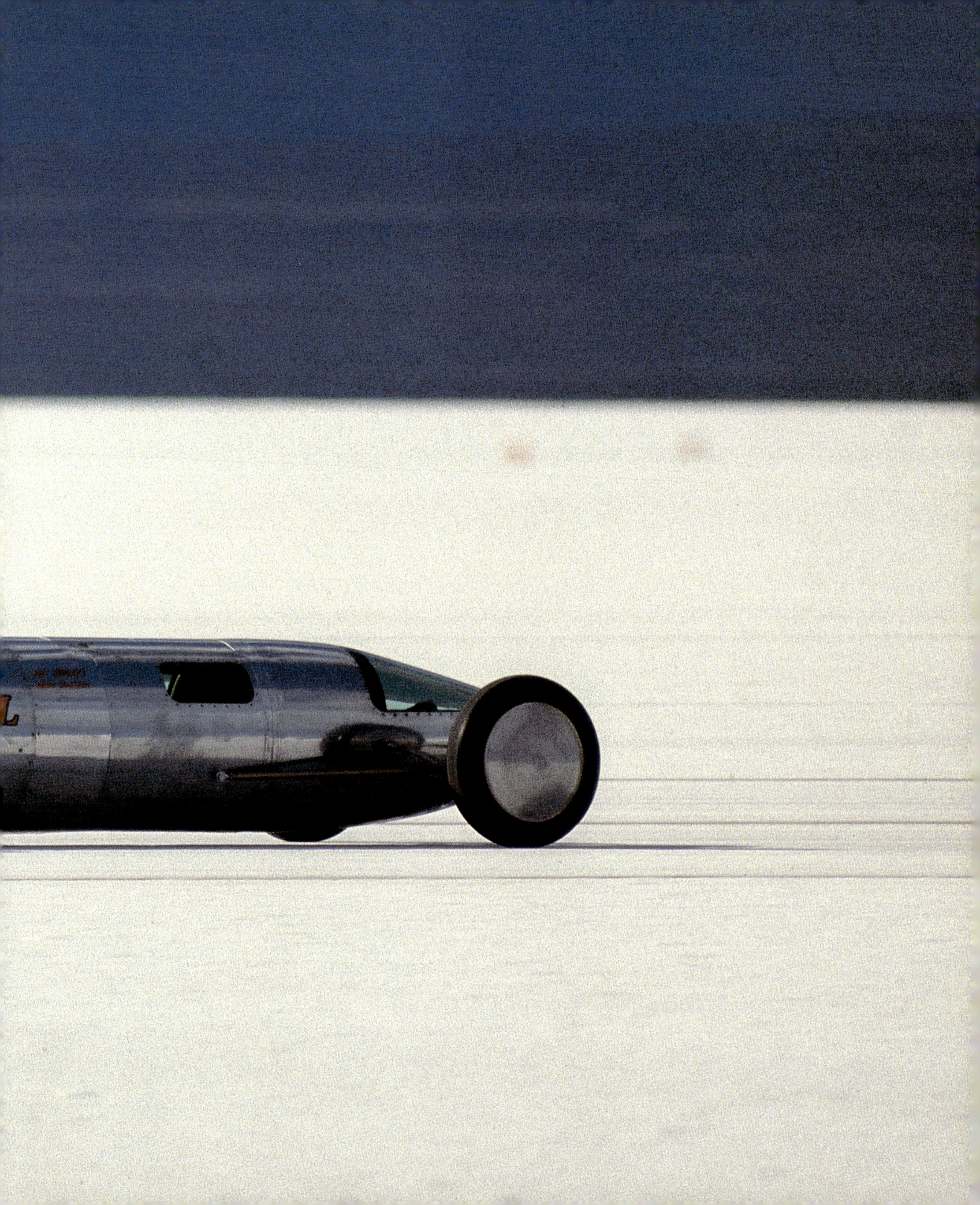

Previous page
An early attempt at streamlining at the salt was to use aircraft belly tanks. Used by P38s in World War II to haul fuel, the tanks unbolted in halves making the addition of framing, engines and cockpit inside the tank easy. Some still run the salt today with the B/Fuel Lakester record of 282.633 mph being held by a drop-tank lakester.

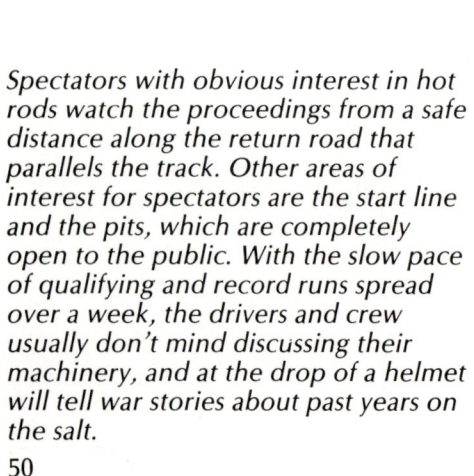

Spectators with obvious interest in hot rods watch the proceedings from a safe distance along the return road that parallels the track. Other areas of interest for spectators are the start line and the pits, which are completely open to the public. With the slow pace of qualifying and record runs spread over a week, the drivers and crew usually don't mind discussing their machinery, and at the drop of a helmet will tell war stories about past years on the salt.

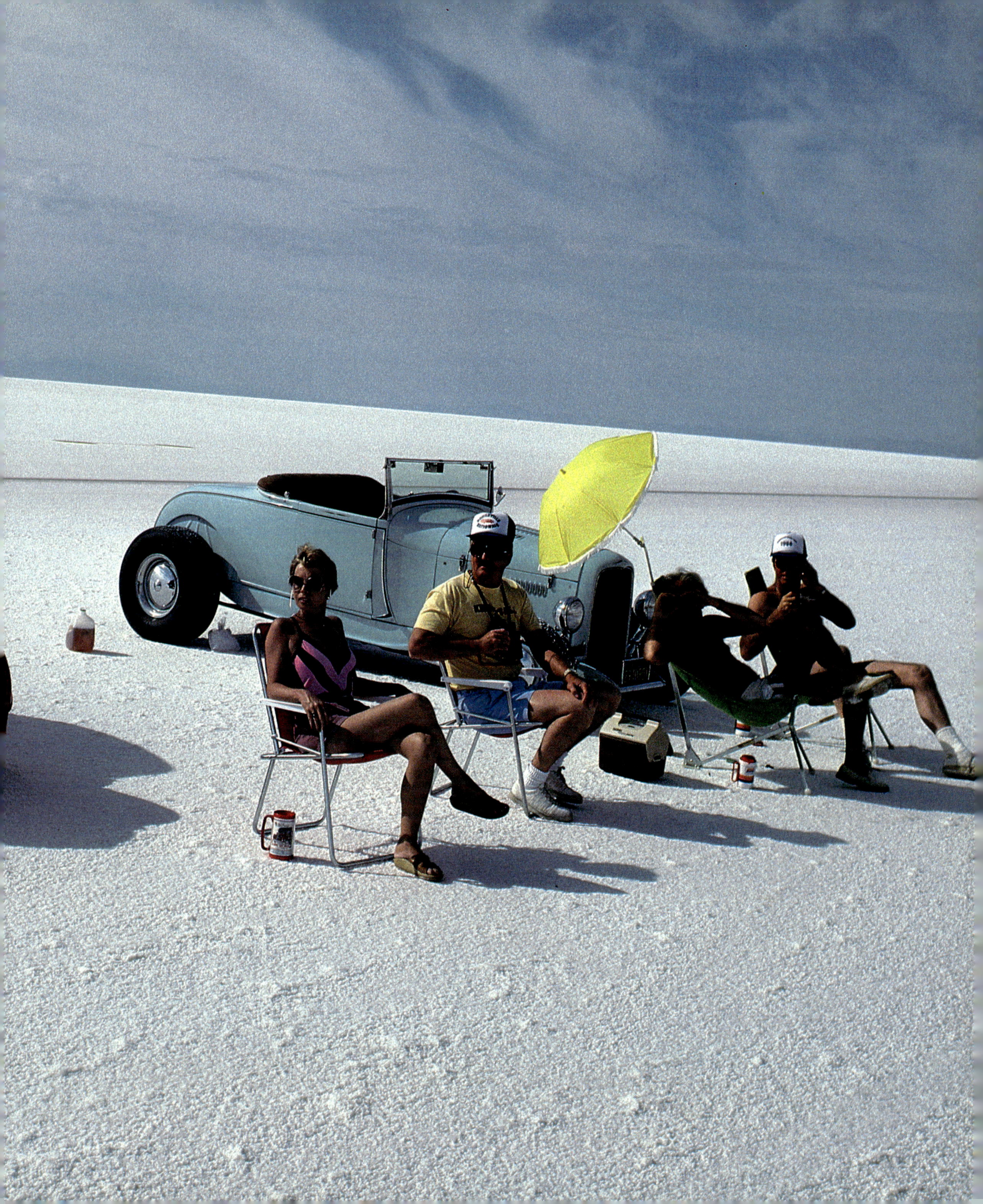

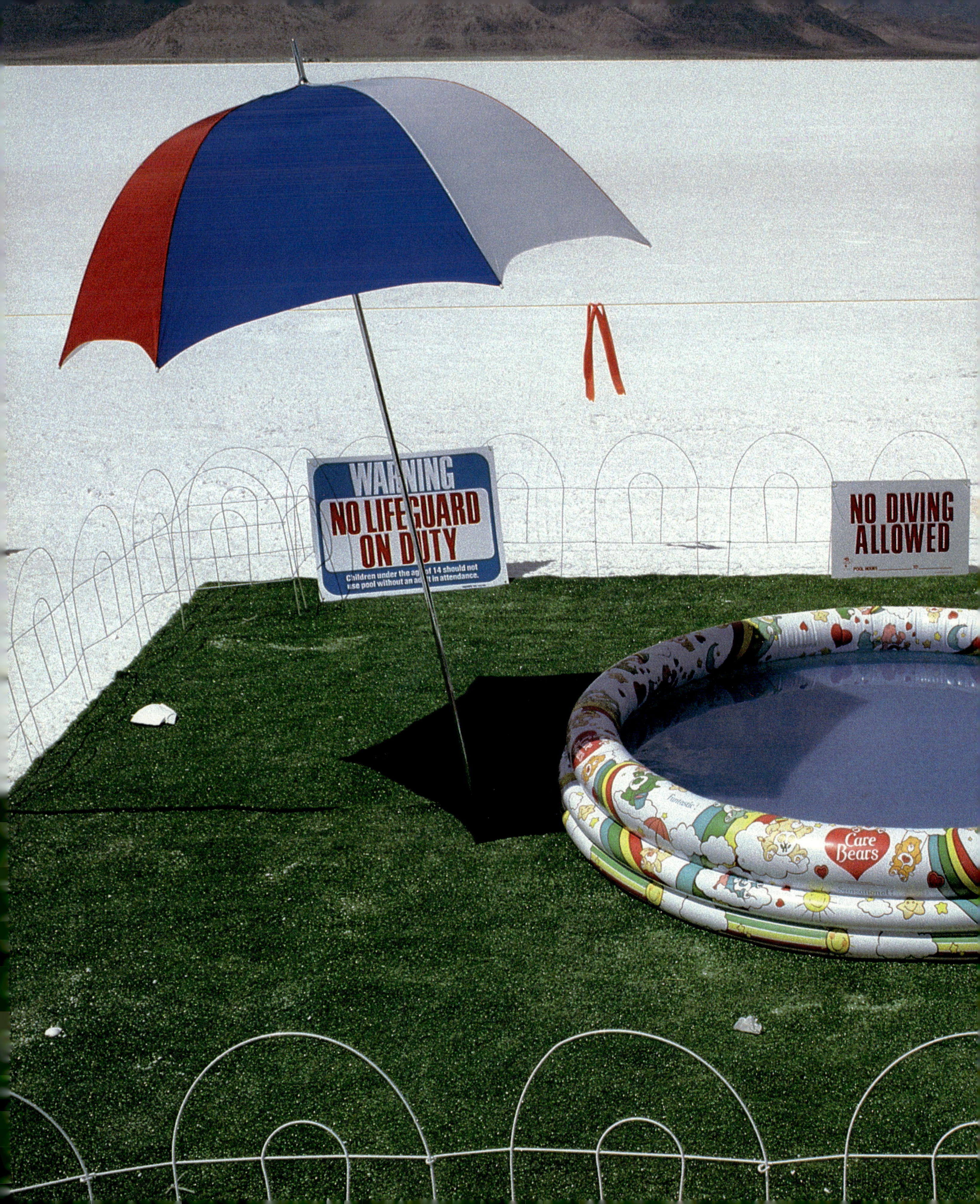
WARNING
NO LIFEGUARD ON DUTY
NO DIVING ALLOWED
Care Bears

A little levity on the warm salt desert that attests to the fact that many racers do bring their families to the salt. A little pool and a motorhome go a long way toward comfort on the salt flats. One group included four families totaling 30 people, many of whom had been coming to Speed Week since 1962. This was their collective planned vacation.

Problems of going fast

The objective of Speed Week is to go faster and faster, but a number of factors control just how fast you can go with a given vehicle.

Power

Horsepower is the fuel for speed, and progressively more power is needed as the speeds increase. In a given car it may take 300 hp to attain 200 mph. To achieve 300 mph in that same vehicle may require about 2,000 hp. The main reason for the disproportionate need for power stems from the wind resistance factor.

Ever increasing power is garnered through larger displacement engines (an 1800 ci engine recently showed up on the salt), supercharging, turbocharging, intercooling and all the ingenuity that hot rodders are known for.

Wind resistance

The faster the vehicle travels, the more the resistance to the wind and the more need for power. Streamlining becomes very critical in designing a vehicle that will go faster. Also to be considered here is the aerodynamics of the body shape. Keeping the frontal area small is of utmost importance. The larger the engine for added power the larger the probable frontal area.

The shape must also be such that downforce on the vehicle helps keep the wheels to the salt for optimum traction. This downforce also robs much of the needed power for the forward speed. It's as though you can't win.

One more consideration is that if the shape of the car forms an airfoil at speed, the vehicle

The big, bad Lincoln Continental makes a point with a bumper sticker. The record for the Lincoln's class (B/Production Sedan/Coupe) is 217.589 mph set by a winged Dodge Charger Daytona. With no hope of reaching those speeds with the heavy Lincoln, everyone on the team was having fun; the car attained a top speed of 164.571 mph. You don't have to break a record to enjoy the salt.

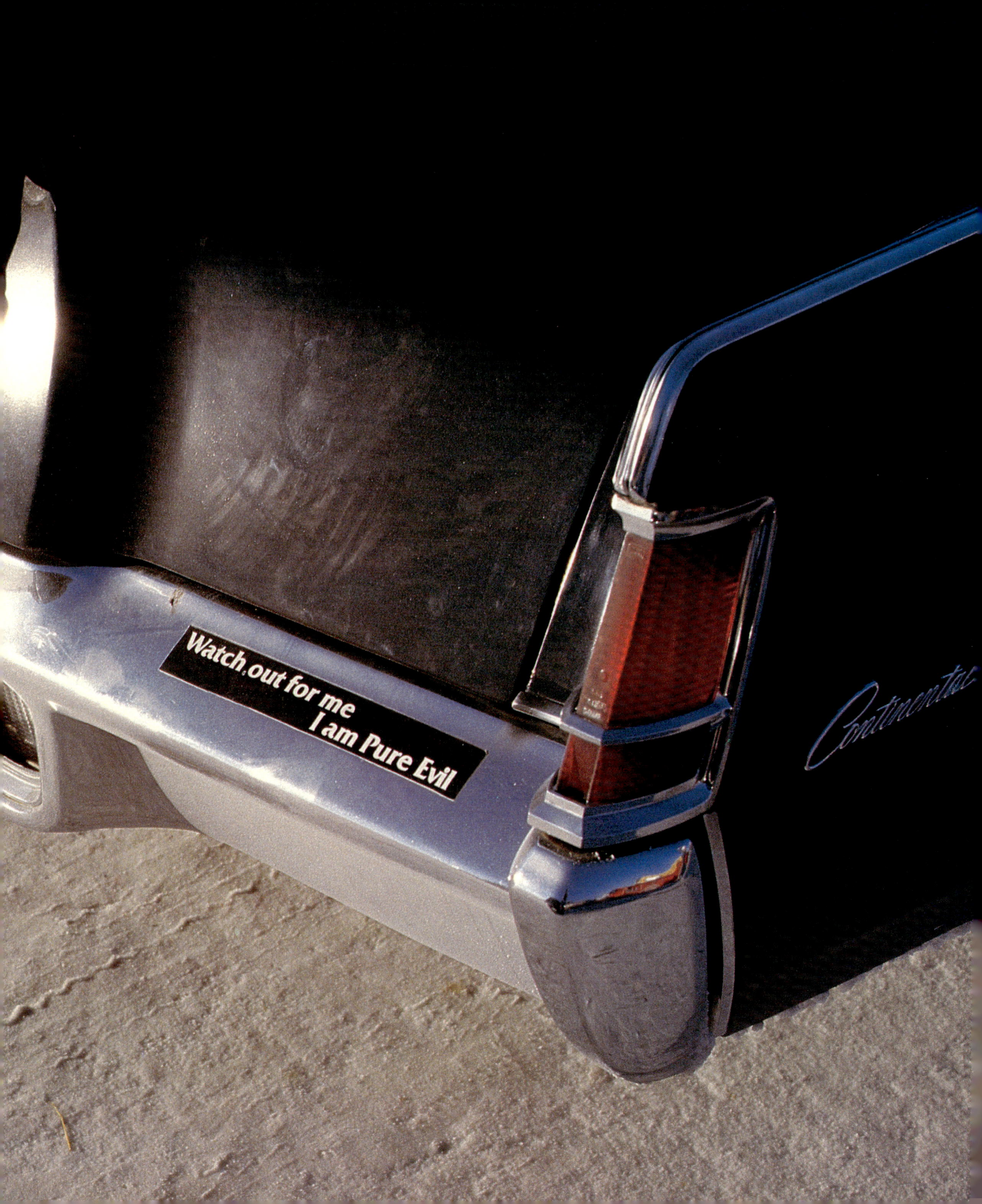
Watch out for me
I am Pure Evil
Continental

may become a disastrously unstable flying machine.

Traction

Having unlimited power to push a vehicle through the air isn't the complete answer. The power has to somehow be transferred to the salt within the length of the track that is available. To make matters worse, the salt is a fairly slick surface. Many of the high-powered cars are still capable of breaking the wheels loose from the salt in top gear at over 200 mph. It takes a controlled and gentle foot on the throttle.

In the past, small tires were used to cut wind resistance, but now the drivers are finding out that a wider tire for traction may be a better compromise. Four-wheel drive is an answer for some vehicles, allowing more power to be applied to the salt. The aerodynamics of downforce on the vehicle body is used, but must be balanced between slowing the forward progress and affecting the handling as the vehicle reaches speed.

BUICK
MOTORSPORTS

Previous page
Salt collects by the exhaust of the V-6 Buick entry. The collecting salt in wheelwells can actually help in streamlining. New racers mistakenly knock off the salt after each run. The salt that collects on hot engine parts, however, will melt onto the metal, making removal difficult.

Beautiful paint and chromed steering assembly of the Pontiac-powered G/Gas Lakester number 51. Various levels of fit and finish are evident on the salt, from salt rust to loving chrome.

This A/Fuel Roadster, run by Leggitt-LaBash-Cook, has disc brakes at the back and no brakes on the front. As long as the drag chutes open, stopping with only back brakes is no problem. The removal of the front brakes is to aid in streamlining. The car had a qualifying time of 251.117 mph.

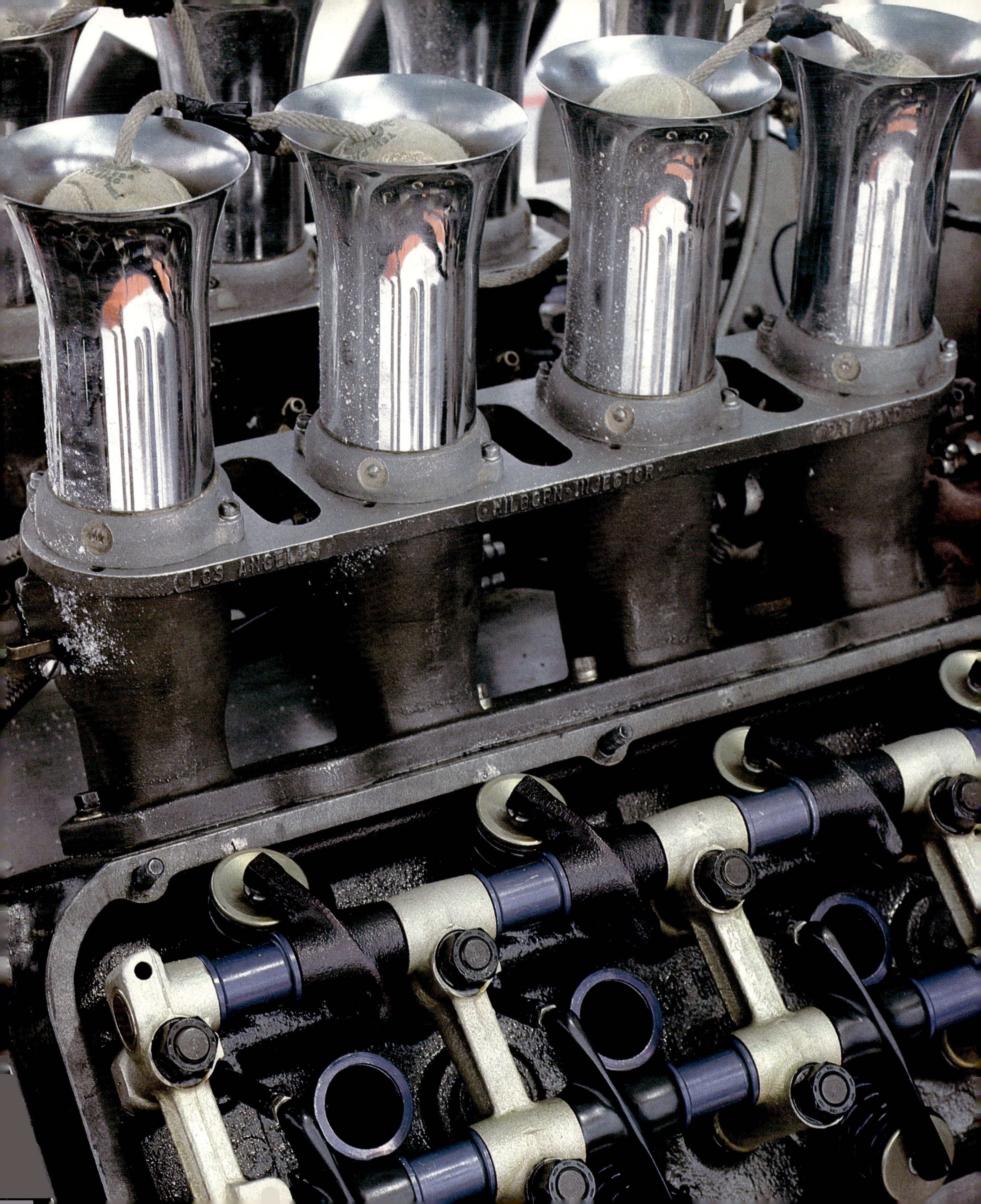
LOS ANGELES
HILBORN INJECTOR

A big-block V-8 with Hilborn injection. The length of the stacks on the injectors is tuned for each engine. Fuel injection, instead of regular carburetion, is a popular method of getting fuel to the engine on the salt because changes are more easily made and the engine runs more efficiently at the higher end. The valve covers are removed from this engine.

A normally aspirated 481 ci Chevrolet with Hilborn port injection powers this B/Altered Pontiac Firebird belonging to Fjastad-Warren. The car came within 4 mph of the class record of 216.392 mph.

A Mooneyman blower sits atop a 510 ci Chevrolet engine in the AA/Gas Roadster number 333 reflecting the colors of the tarps that afford the only shade on the warm Bonneville Salt Flats.

A/Street Roadster number 74 with a Chevy engine and turbocharger. Turbochargers offer the advantage of not taking away from the engine's horsepower to run them. A supercharger/blower hooks directly to the engine's camshaft, robbing it of some of the increased power.

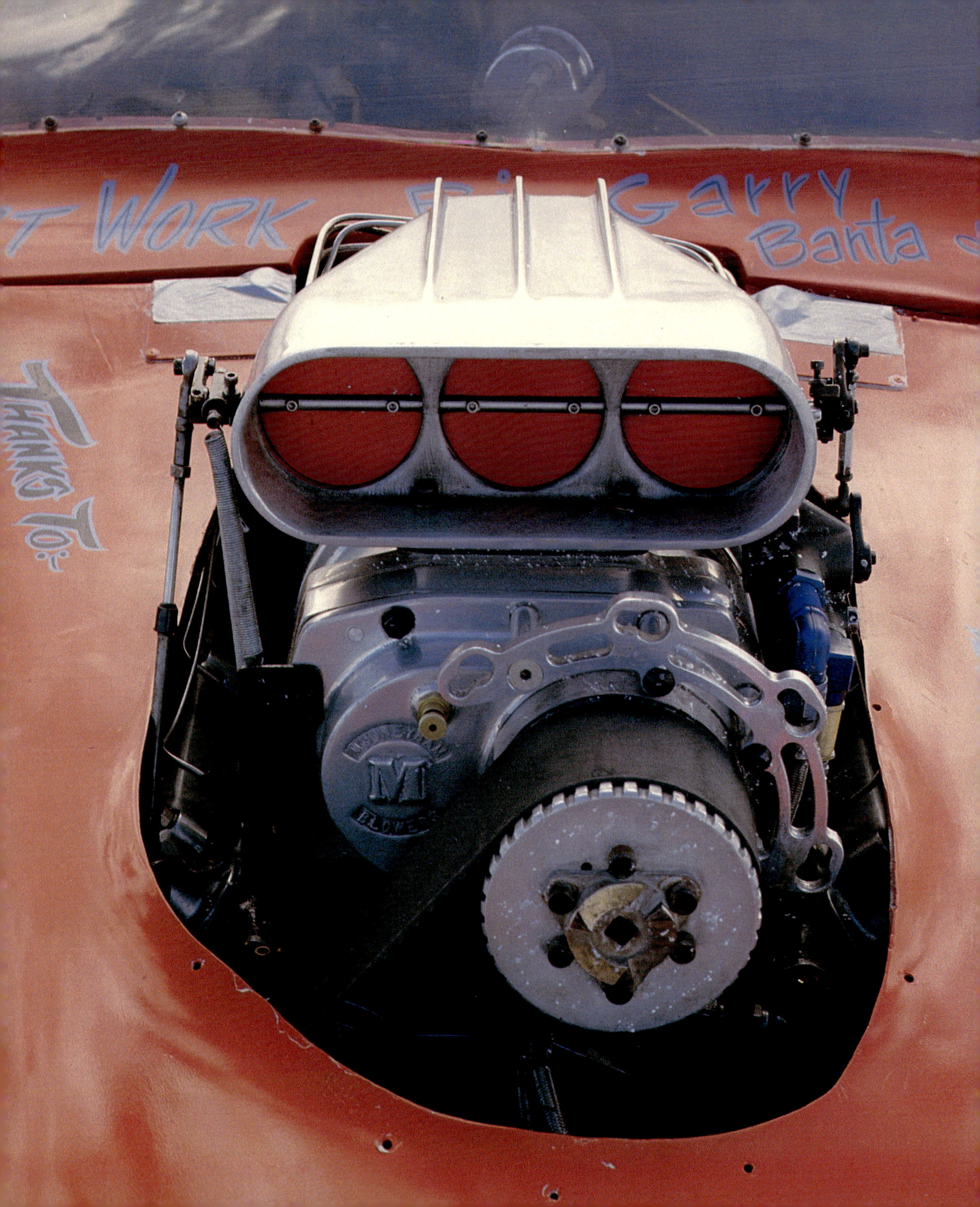
WORK
Garry
Banta
THANKS TO:

A Mooneyman blower pokes through the hood. Similar to the General Motors blowers on diesel trucks, this Roots-type blower compresses the air before it enters the engine. The blower is run directly off the engine shaft versus the turbochargers that run off the air from the engine's exhaust.

The remains of an engine that blew up on a run down the salt. The sustained loads placed on the engines as they travel the five miles under full power can have the end result shown here. Engines of greater power are used in drag racing, but they only need to maintain the power for about eight seconds. At the Bonneville Salt Flats, a full-power run may last two minutes. Many racers have broken the record on their first run, only to end up at the seven-mile marker without an engine for the return run needed to establish the record.

Next page
A summer thunderstorm scatters the racers and sends them back to the pits and hotels in Wendover, Nevada. After a good dousing, the salt may take as long as two days before it dries out enough to race on. A second storm can cancel the remainder of the meet.

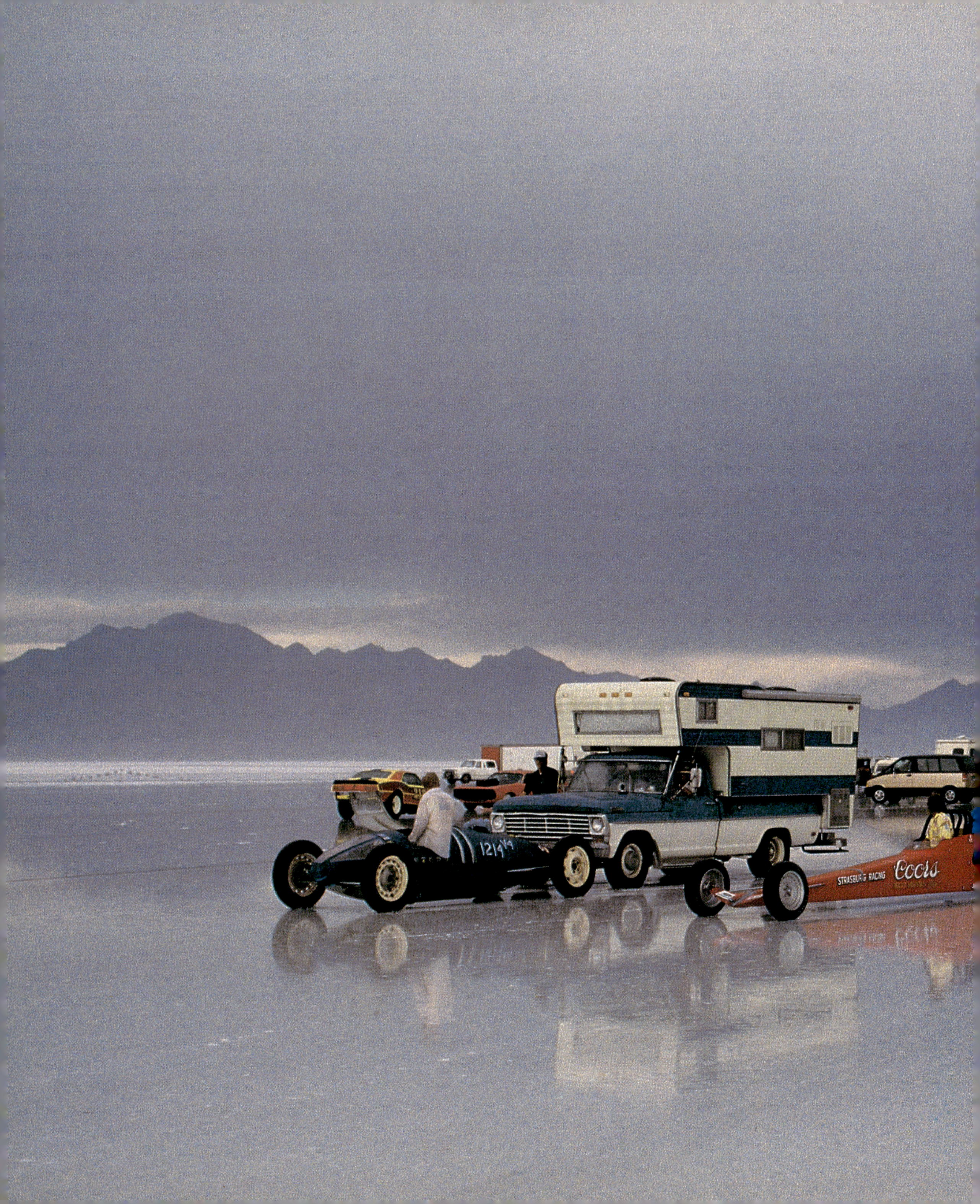
STRASBURG RACING
Coors

The results of spinning a roadster at nearly 200 mph. With the slick salt and the car's low center of gravity a spin is usually harmless, except to the tires, which end up shredding. The longer, narrower streamliners and lakesters must be careful not to get sideways, as the result can be a pencil-roll—a disastrous tumble with the possibility of flipping end over end.

This Chevrolet Camaro with a 475 ci engine spins its wheels as it tries to get the power to the salt. Maintaining a link between the vehicle's wheels and the salt surface is one of the major problems in getting the added power to equate to added speed. Some cars run wider tires for traction, while others opt for narrow tires to minimize air drag.

Classes

You can't tell the players without a program, and the diversity of the race cars and bikes is great. The smallest vehicle that can be remembered to have competed on the salt was a tiny streamliner with a 3 ci engine rolling on bicycle tires. The largest was brought to the salt by a gentleman by the name of Graham. It contained an Allison aircraft engine displacing 2000 ci. Recently a lakester with an 1800 ci tank engine tried a run down the track, but after one attempt the driver was looking for a stronger transmission.

The following is a generalized description of each category for cars and motorcycles. The vehicles are also often separated by whether they use exotic fuel mixtures or standard pump gasoline. Many more rules apply than are listed here, but this will give you an idea of the cast of characters that speed down the "long black line."

Car classes

Special construction

This is the top of the categories in aerodynamics and, ultimately, speed. More than one engine can be used, and either fuel or gas is allowed depending on the class. No production bodies are allowed. The only other restrictions in this class have to do with safety.

Streamliner/FS (fuel), GS (gas). These are the all-out record cars. Four wheels are required but they need not be in a regular rectangular configuration. The only restriction of the design of the body is that at least two wheels must be covered. The Speed Week overall record is more than 354 mph. The record for any wheel-driven car (streamliner) on the salt flats is 409.277 mph set by the Summers brothers' *Goldenrod* in November 1965.

Lakester/FL (fuel), GL (gas). Included are all open-wheeled cars with only one engine. Some of the cars incorporate the classic P-28 drop tank,

Jeff Carroll Racing's E/Gas Lakester speeding down the track. The lakester has a 257 ci Buick V-6 engine and turned a speed of 211 mph, 15 mph below the record.

7306E/GL
R.J. CARROLL
& SONS PLUMBING
SPECIALTY
METAL FABRICATION
EAST VALLEY GARAGE
AVIAID
VALVOLINE
BUICK

while others look very much like dragsters, but are designed to go far beyond just a quarter mile. Top speed in these classes is 318+ mph.

Vintage

This category is specifically for the "antique iron" that still exists out there. The bodies must be early American production cars built prior to 1948 (at least 500 made) or exact replicas of the original, with aluminum and fiberglass allowed. The safety features in these cars must meet current standards. These are the epitome of the American hot rod of years past.

Modified Roadster/FMR (fuel), GMR (gas). The ultimate roadster class still uses an exact reproduction, from the firewall back, of a roadster body produced prior to 1939. The engine may be set back fifty percent of the wheelbase, and the driver's seat may be at any location between the firewall and the rear axle. Streamlining is allowed ahead of the cowl, but no coverings of the wheels and tires are allowed. The fastest attained speed in these classes is just over 276 mph.

Fuel-Gas Roadster/FR (fuel), GR (gas). These cars must have production or exact replica bodies of roadsters from between 1928 and 1938. These classes have been around the longest, with updating of safety features only. A few simple modifications can be done, but overall, these cars haven't changed much from the roadsters racing on dry lakes in the thirties. Top speed in these classes is 250+ mph.

Street Roadster/ST-R (gas). Bodies here must be pre-1938 with all stock panels except hood side panels, front fenders and running boards. The driver must sit in the original position. Also required are a horn, taillights, headlights and a full transmission. The car must be capable of self-starting. All of the above amenities are designed to make the car street legal. The record for the top of these classes is just over 195 mph.

Vintage Competition Coupe, Vintage Coupe and Sedan, Vintage Altered Coupe (fuel and gas). The rules in these classes are identical to the respective modified classes, except that only 1948 or earlier bodies with small or V-4 engines are allowed. Turbochargers are not allowed.

Modified

Competition Coupe and Sedan/FCC (fuel), GCC (gas). This is as fast as they get with doors and a roof. A production coupe or sedan body that is unaltered in width or contour, yet can be chopped, channeled, bellypanned and have streamlining ahead of and including the cowl qualifies. Top speed for these classes is an ear-shattering 237+ mph.

Fuel Coupe and Sedan/FC (fuel), Gas Altered Coupe and Sedan/ALT (gas). One step down from competition coupes, these bodies are 1928 or later and must remain in their original configuration with no streamlining allowed. The fuel used determines the class. Gas runs in the altered class, while those using fuel are designated to the fuel group. A little over 245 mph is tops for these cars.

Gas Coupe and Sedan/GC (gas). Vehicles in this class are to be representative of typical street machines in that they do run on gas, must be in stock configuration and have all-street-legal equipment. This equipment includes headlights, taillights, horn and so on. In the past, the favorite car for this class has been the streamlined Studebaker designed by Raymond Loewy in the early fifties, but in recent years late-model Camaros and Firebirds have dominated the record book. The top record in this class is presently held by a Firebird with a speed in excess of 268 mph.

Modified Sports/MS (gas). Production sports cars that have been modified to the extent of not being eligible for Production class or have bodies of limited production (such as Devin, Kellison and Bradley) fall into this category. No streamlining is allowed, but superchargers and turbochargers are. Records in this class are up to 244 mph.

Production

This category consists of vehicles that could be purchased at a dealership and driven home. No aerodynamic modifications to the vehicle and no parts which are not part of that vehicle's production run are allowed.

Production Coupe and Sedan/PROD (gas). This group incorporates American and foreign coupes, sedans and pickups (with full stock beds) that are unaltered in height, width and contour. They must have all-stock panels mounted in original relationship to one another. A production run of at least 500 vehicles must have been made. The top speed turned by a production coupe or sedan is 219+ mph.

Production-Supercharged P/S. These vehicles meet the same requirements as the production coupes and sedans, but are equipped with factory supercharger systems. The only record in this class so far was turned by a Dodge Shelby Charger at 171+ mph.

Grand Touring Sport/GT (gas). Here we have the sporty cars. The body must be of the original configuration and street legal. The cars do not have rear seats that would allow continued adult occupancy. Engine swaps are allowed so long as the engine is the same make as the body. Supercharging is legal and gas is the only fuel allowed. Top speed record for the sporty cars is 240+ mph.

Diesel Truck/DT. Diesel trucks with a capacity of up to one ton and having unaltered bodies (American or foreign manufactured) make up this class. Engine and driveline swaps are permitted. The diesel truck record stands at 159+ mph.

Highway Hauler/HH (diesel, two-axle/ three-axle). American and foreign production diesel-powered trucks of not less than 14,500 lb., unaltered in height, width and contour, and capable of hauling freight make up this class. The fastest highway hauler to date exceeded 132 mph.

Motorcycle classes

Motorcycles are classed according to a combination of frame type, engine type and engine displacement. Speeds range from the record 82+ mph in the 50 cc group to the record 231+ mph in the 3000 cc group. The fastest of the motorcycles are the streamliners, with a top speed of 318+ mph achieved by Don Vesco in 1978 with a displacement of 3000 cc.

Frame

Production F/P. A standard production road motorcycle must have at least 500 produced and be available for sale to the general public.

Modified F/M. These frames must be based on the original equipment frame. This class includes factory-produced road racing and off-road motorcycles of which less than 200 were produced.

Class A F/A. The frame is unlimited in design, except that streamlining is not permitted. It must be driven by the rear wheels only and may have two or three wheels.

Streamliner/S. A streamliner is a motorcycle designed so that it is not possible to see the complete rider in the normal riding position from either side or from above. The wheelbase is unlimited and must make a single track. The power will be to the rear wheel, and steering must be done with the front wheels only.

Sidecars/SC. A sidecar is a three-wheeled vehicle leaving two tracks with only the rear-most wheel driving. All sidecars must have a passenger for stability.

Engine

Production/P. Production engines must be the same model as the model frame being used and must have a stock external appearance. Carburetors must be the same model and size as the original equipment, and the starter mechanism must be retained and operable.

Production Supercharged/PS. Same requirements as production, but an original brand, factory-installed turbocharger or supercharger can be used.

AF. Major parts of the engine must be components designed primarily for use in motorcycle engines; otherwise design is unlimited. No restrictions on fuel. Superchargers and turbochargers are not permitted.

AG. Same as class AF except it is limited to pump gasoline.

ABF. Same as class AF except supercharger or turbocharger is required and must be mechanically or exhaust driven. No restrictions on fuel.

ABG. Same as ABF class except limited to pump gasoline.

VG and VF. Same as class AG and AF except the class is limited to motorcycle engines produced prior to 1957.

Displacement

Combined with frame type and engine type, the last consideration for class placement is the cubic centimeter displacement of the engine. The following is the breakdown of those categories in cubic centimeters: 50, 100, 125, 175, 250, 350, 500, 650, 750, 1000, 1300, 2000 and 3000.

240
FUEL LAKESTER
Carr
NGK
JOHN GATES
FRANK
DAVIS CARS
MORGAN
CALIF. CHASSIS Engr.
VELASCO'S
ENGINE Dynamics
CIRELLO

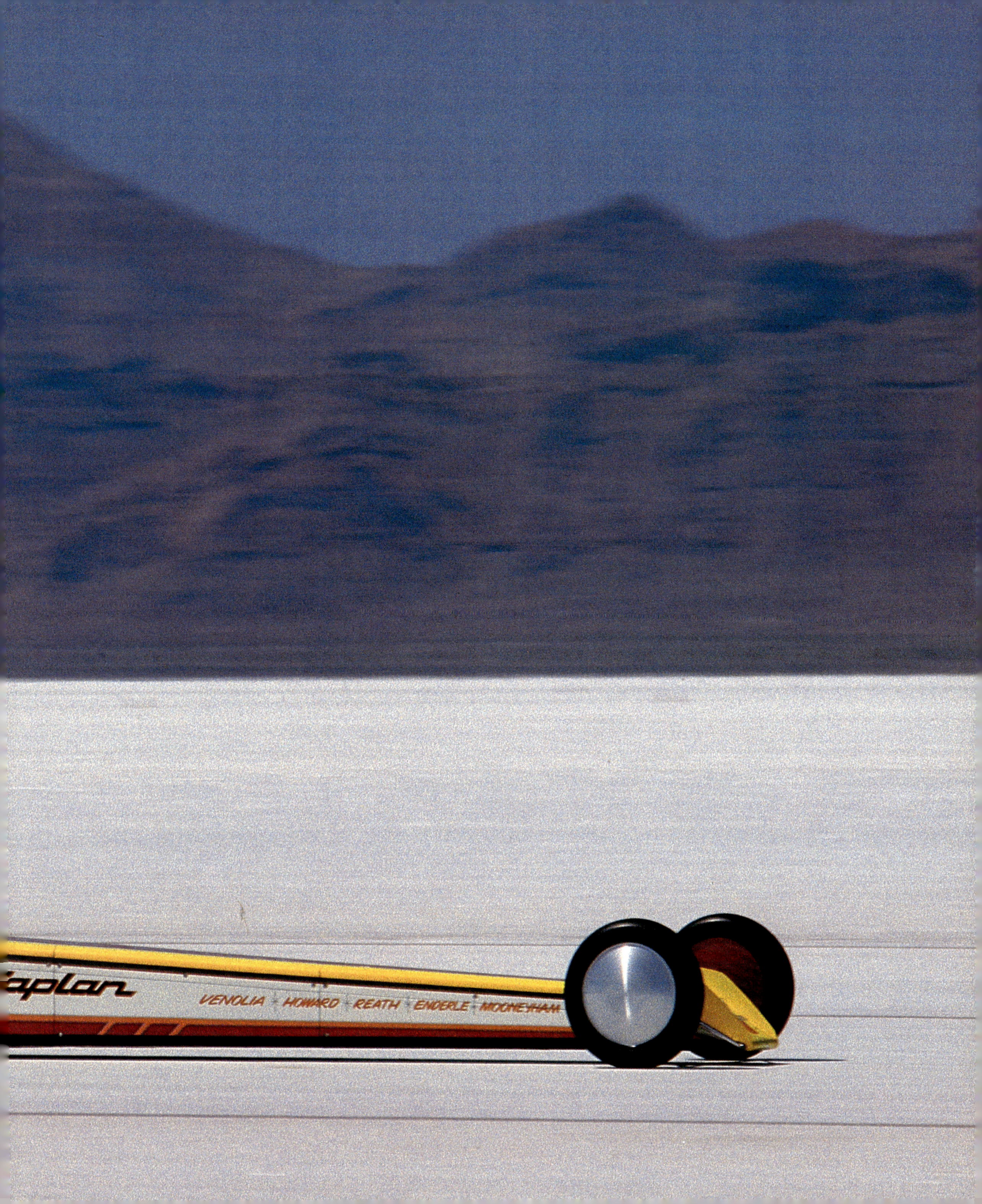
VENOLIA HOWARD REATH ENDERLE MOONEYHAM

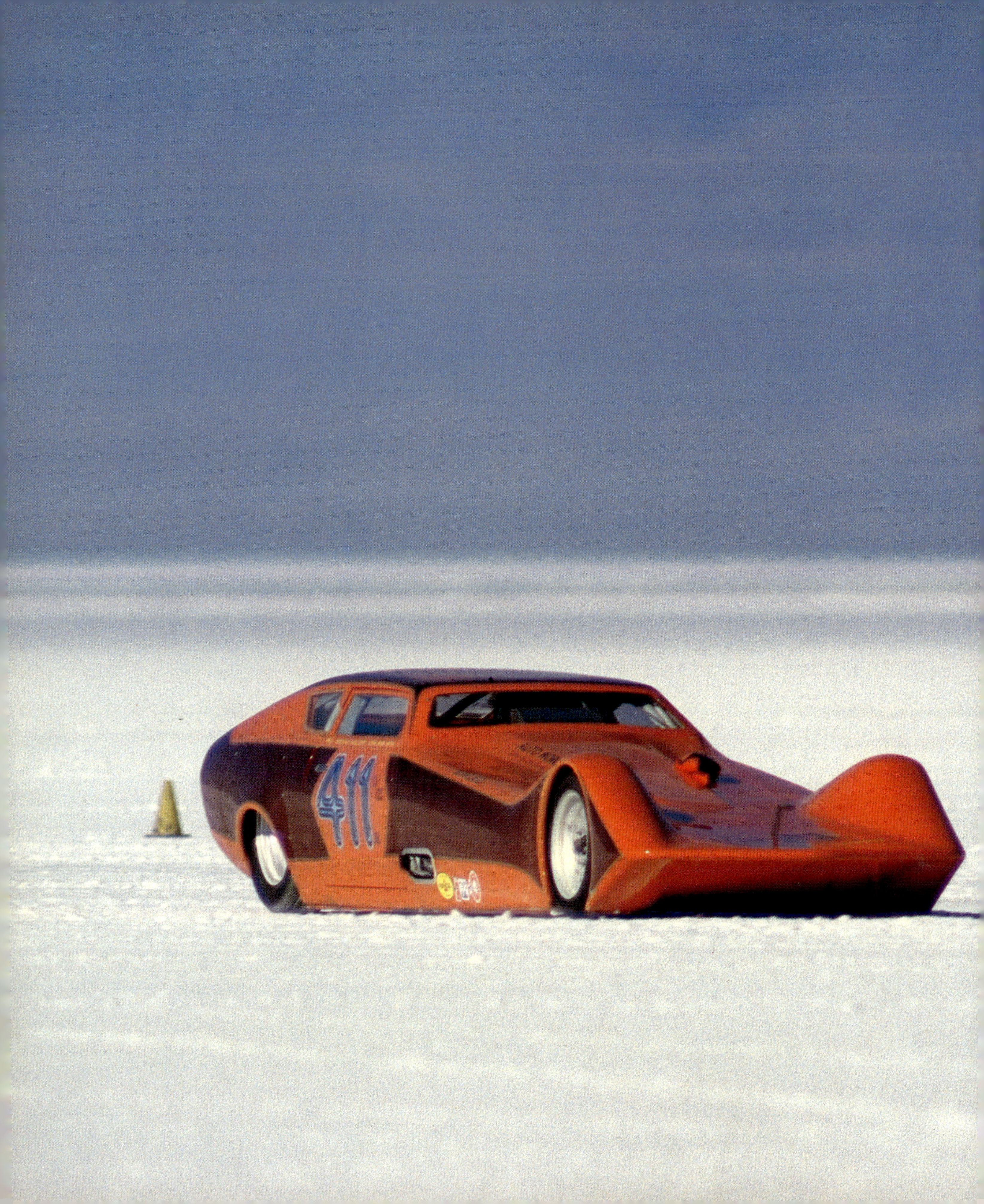
411

Previous page
The fastest of the lakesters that look like quarter-mile rail dragsters is the 440 ci hemi-powered AA/Fuel Lakester of Carr-Kaplan. Unlike the drag strip, where the engine needs to only last for a few seconds, on the salt the engine must power the car for at least five miles and possibly do it twice in the period of an hour. Driver Don Carr holds the lakester record at 318.483 mph. Also included in the lakester class are the belly tank cars that were very popular after World War II. Some of these cars still race at Speed Week.

This D/Fuel Competition Coupe was derived from a 1975 Datsun B-210. The car had a one-way record run at 209+ mph, against the record of 205 mph, but because it was not able to make a return run, no record was broken.

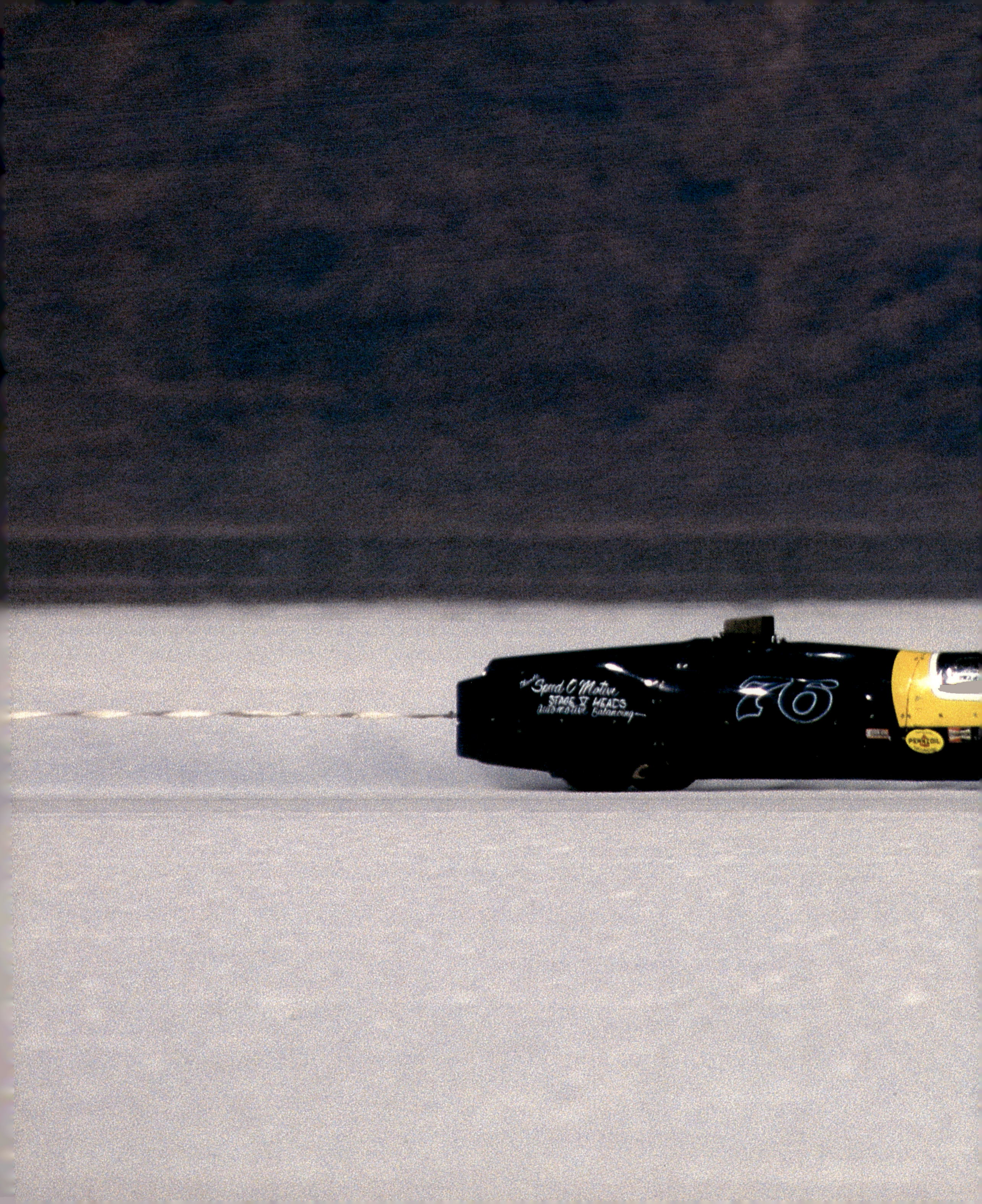
Speed O Motive
STAGE V HEADS
76
PENNZOIL

Previous page
One of the fastest vehicles on the salt is the Speed-O-Motive of Al Teague. Al drove the car to a new B/Fuel Streamliner record of 349.695 mph.

The AA/Fuel Three Wheeler of Clupper Racing is a highly modified motorcycle with 2000 cc of engine. The driver, Charles Clupper, has a different view of the salt and the black line as he heads down the track for a run of 182+ mph.

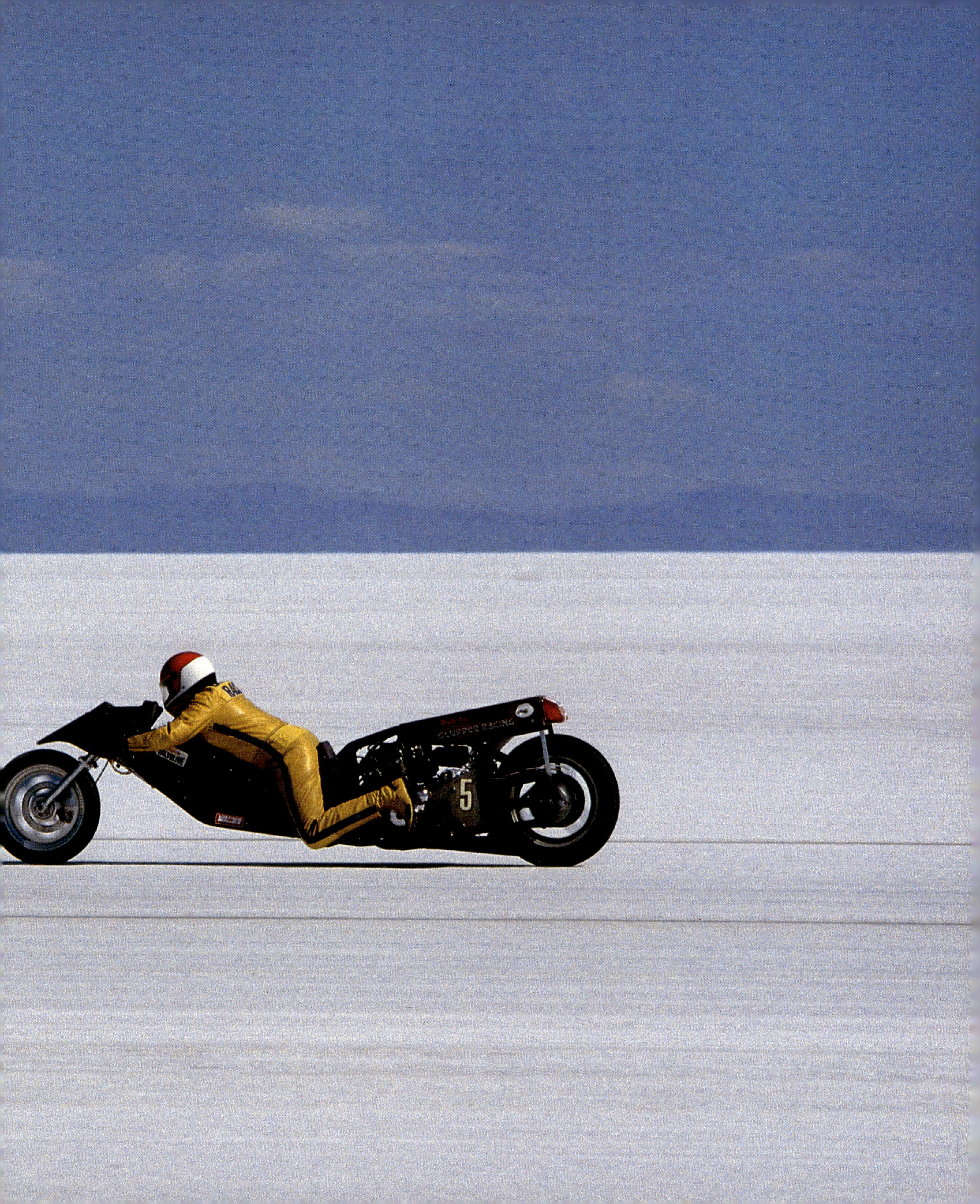
5

The Dodge Charger Daytona Fly Rod *set a B/Altered Coupe record of 216.392 mph. The streamlined Daytona was originally built for NASCAR speedway races in the sixties. The sloped nose and wing work well at the speeds necessary on the salt, and several of the cars are competitive during Speed Week.*

SYKES & FREDERICK'S
Fly Rod
CREW
PETE WEIS
ROSS SHERBURN
BUCKY FUCHS
MARK LYNCH
ARIAS
VALVOLINE
707

The Wheel Center Vette is an A/Modified Sports that qualified at a new record of 215.126 mph against a record of 210, only to have a competitor break that speed with a record run of 218.930. Sometimes you're not only racing against the record, but also the other cars in your class.

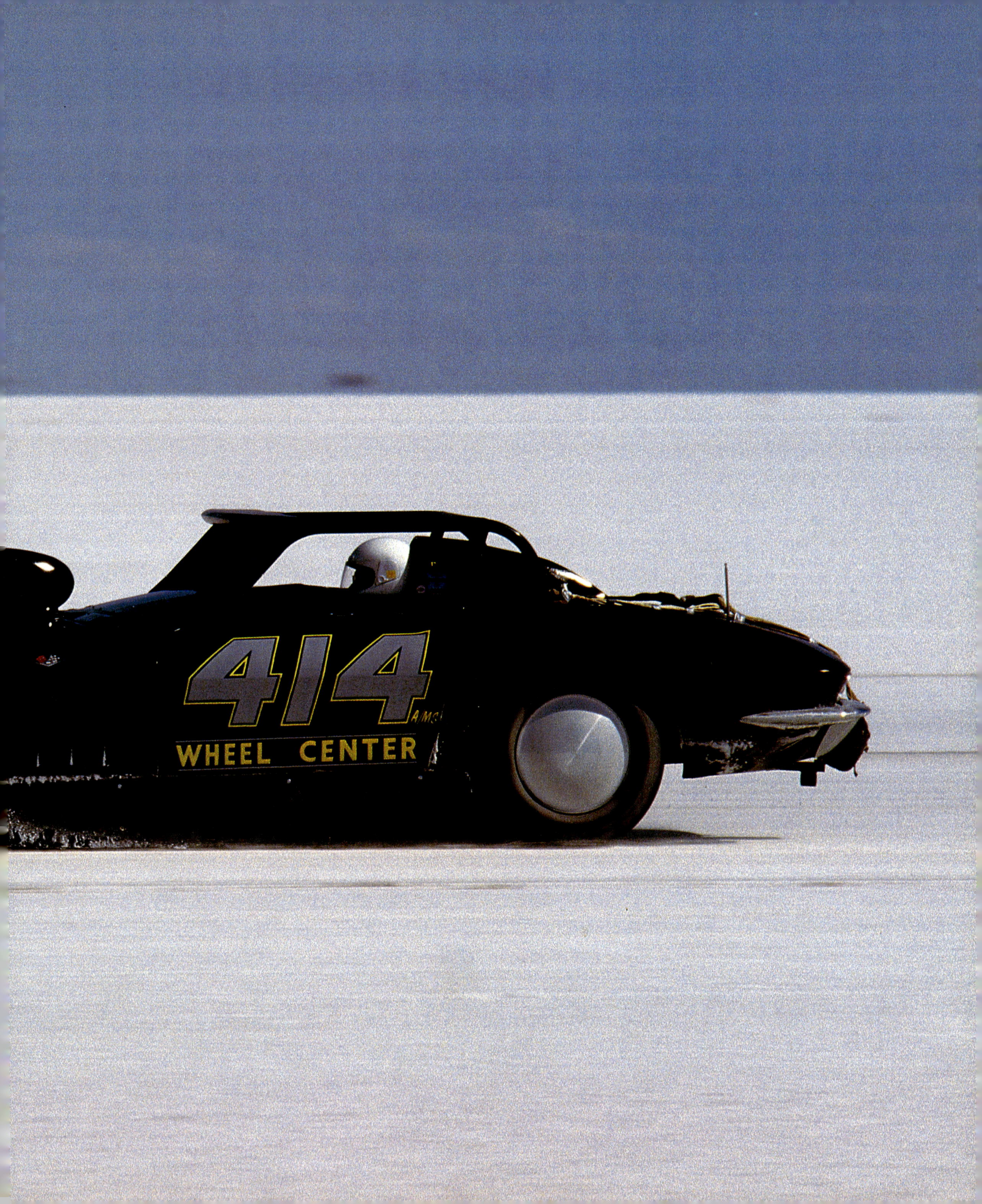
414
WHEEL CENTER

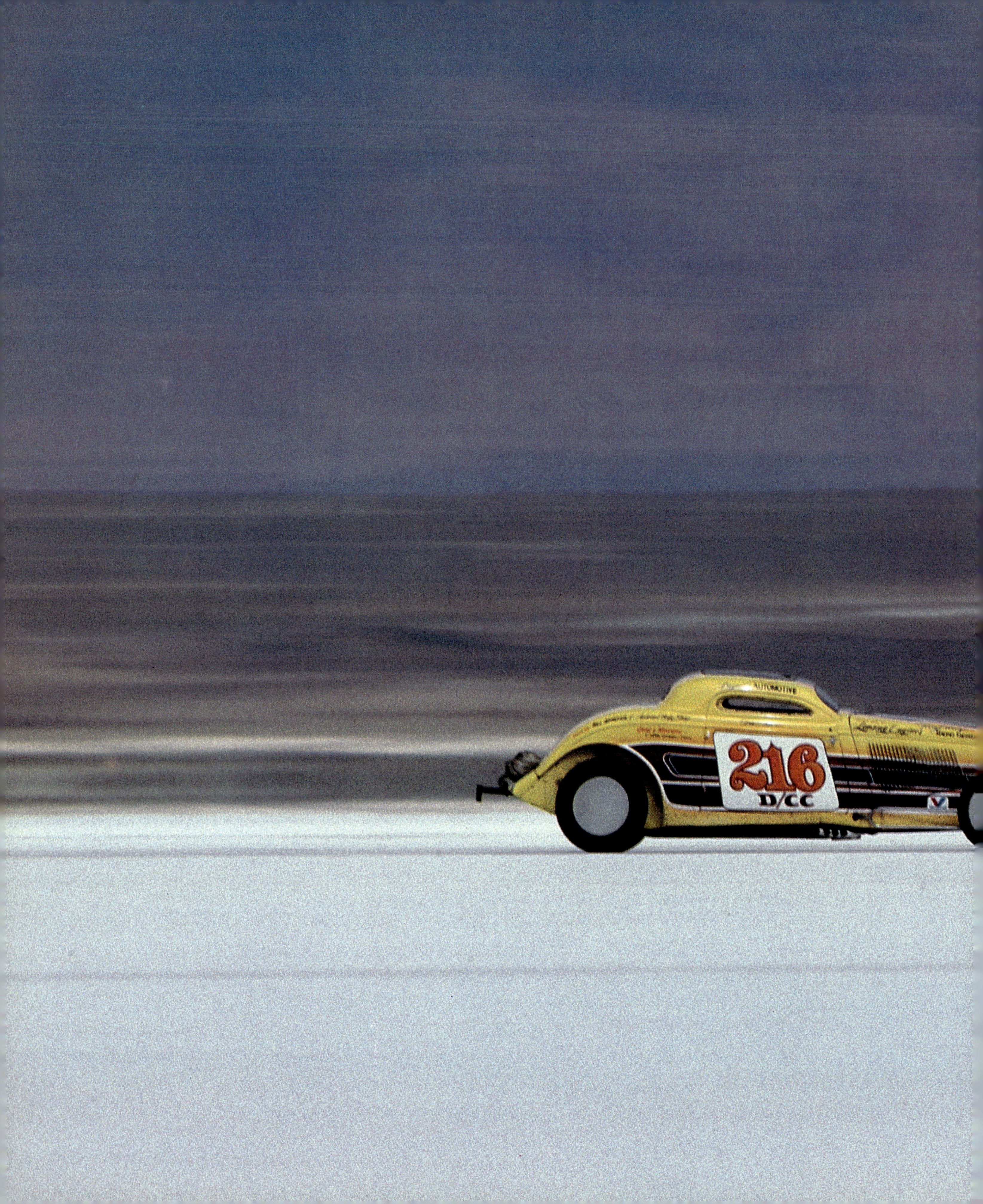
AUTOMOTIVE
216
D/CC

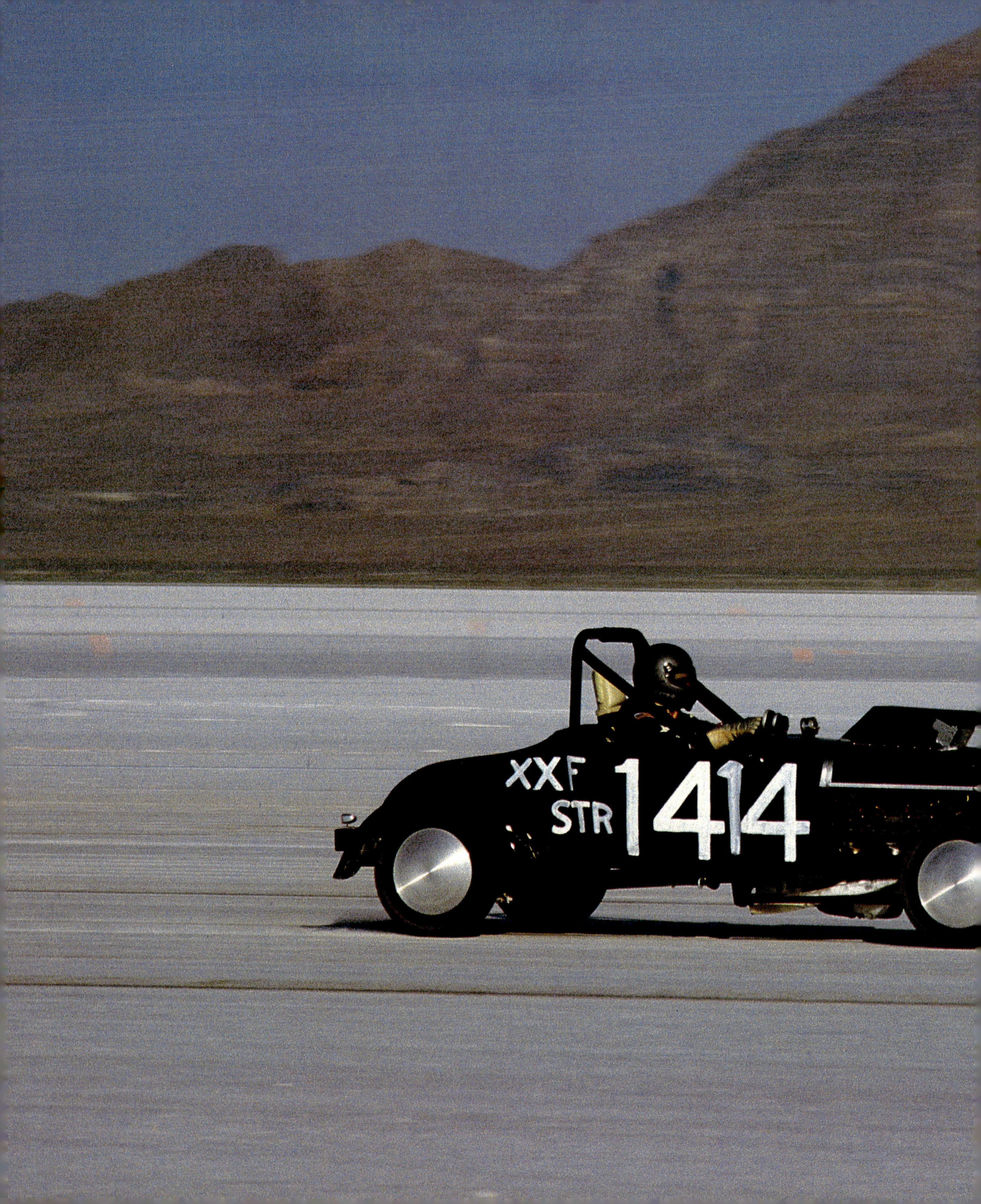
XXF
STR
1414

Previous page
The Tom Thumb Special III *is a real throwback to the hot rods that raced on the salt in the forties and fifties. It runs in D/Fuel Competition Coupe where the top can be chopped and streamlining is allowed ahead of and including the cowl. The* Tom Thumb Special III *with its 304 ci Chevrolet engine had a best speed of 200.177 mph.*

The Hayseed Special *competed in two classes by running first as an XF/Street Roadster and later in the week as an XX/Street Roadster by adding a blower to the engine. Street roadsters are also typical of the street rods of the forties and fifties with the added items to make them street legal: headlights, taillights, horn and so on.*

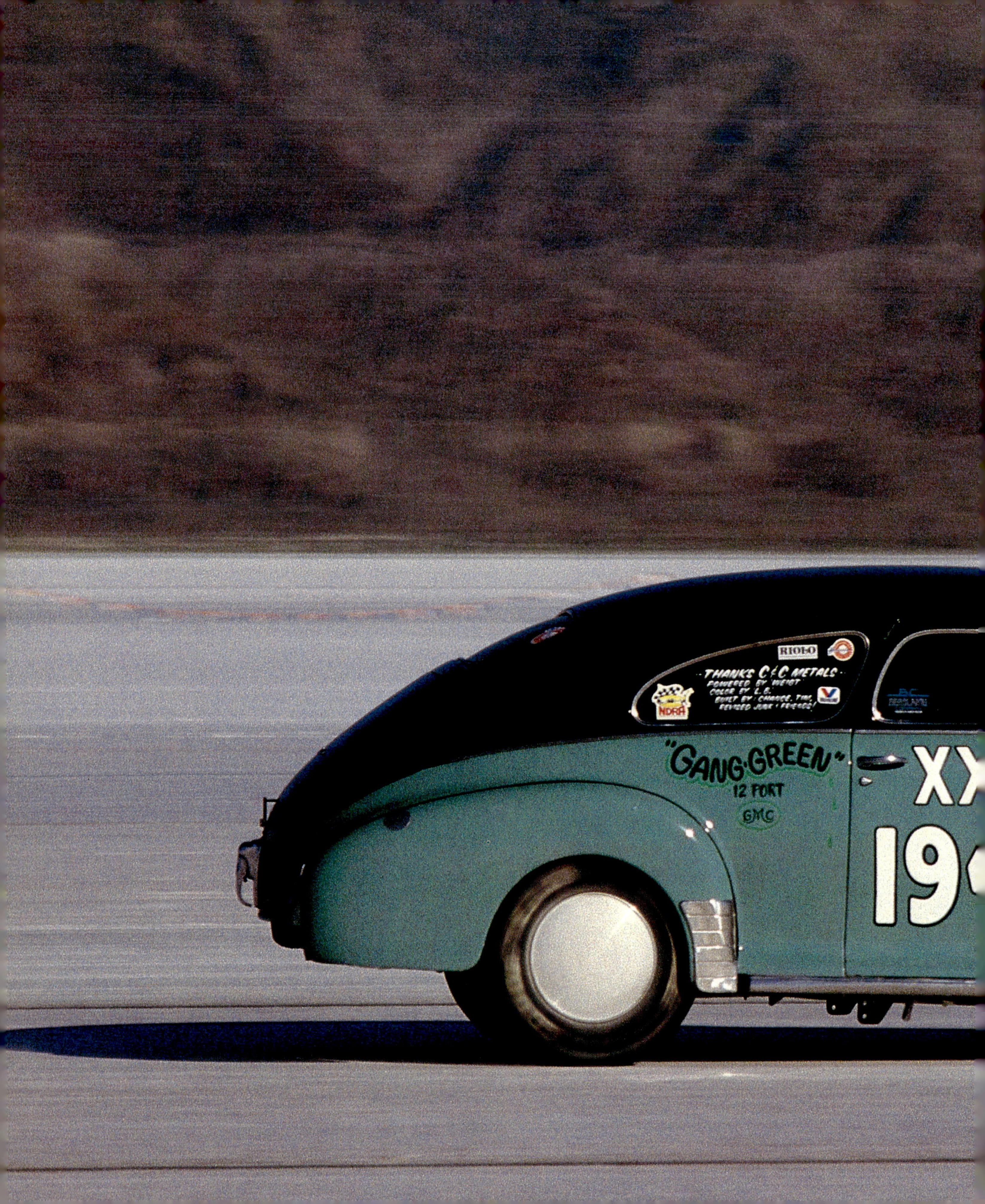
RIOLO
THANKS C&C METALS
NDRA
"GANG·GREEN"
12 PORT
GMC
XX
19

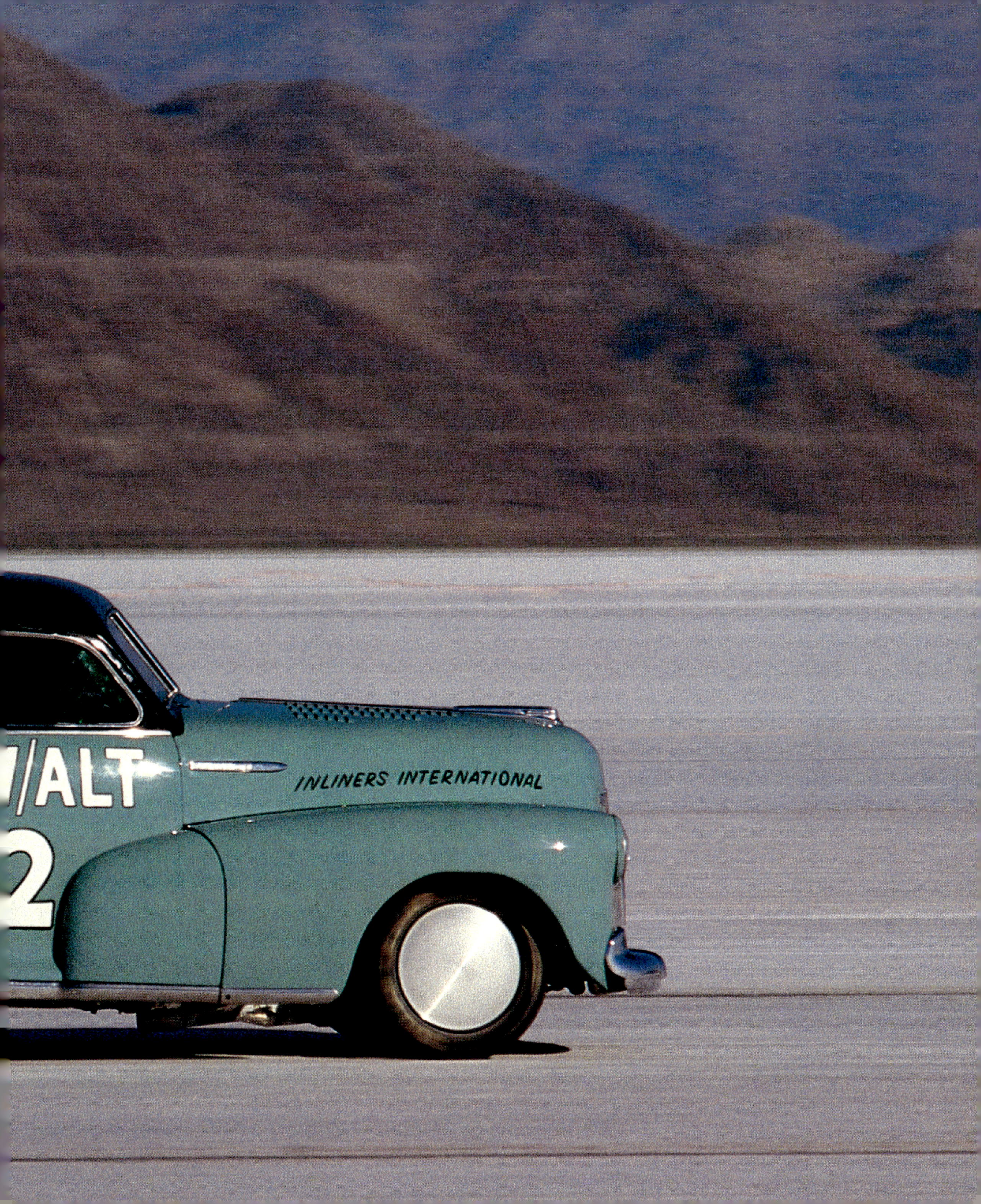
/ALT
INLINERS INTERNATIONAL

Previous page
Not the sleekest, lightest, newest entry at the salt, but a record breaker none the less. This 1942 XX/Vintage Altered Coupe set a record of 150.006 mph.

A recent addition to the car classes on the salt is the Vintage Oval Track racers. When a new class is established a committee determines the minimum speed needed for a new record. Oval racer number 911 starts down the salt to try to establish that new record.

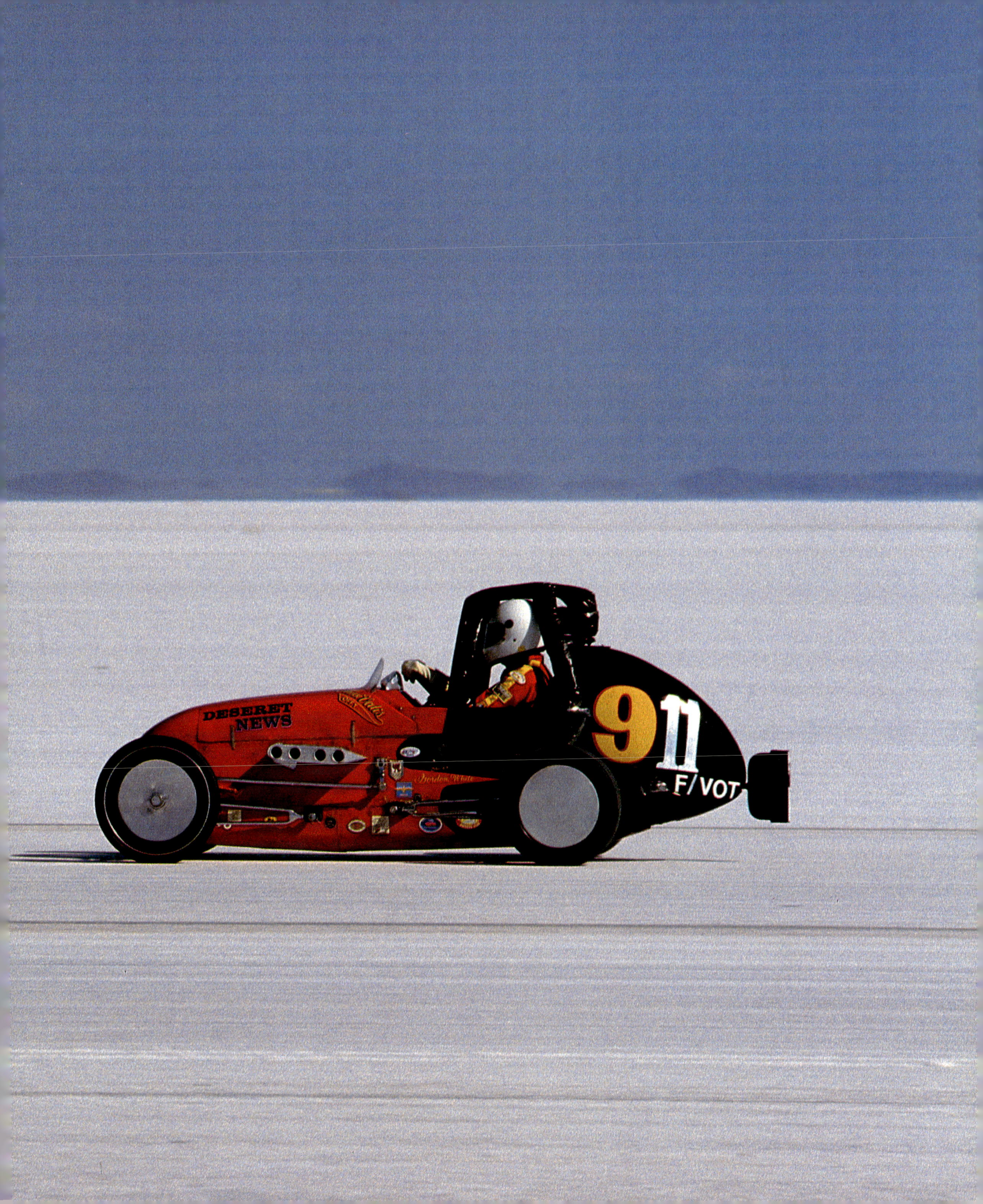
DESERET
NEWS
911
F/VOT

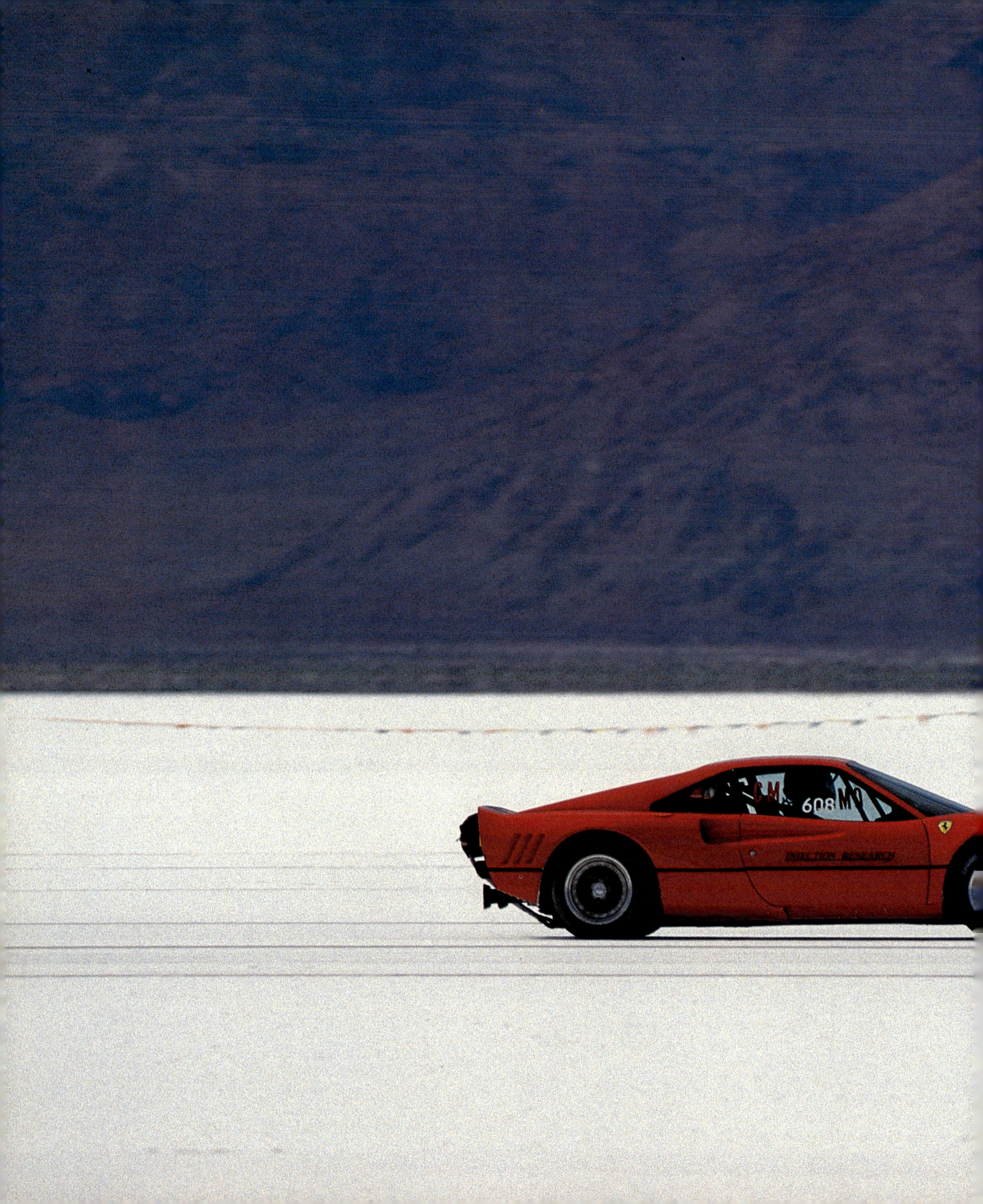
608
INJECTION RESEARCH

The Ferrari-Chevrolet of Bob Norwood starting a qualifying run that would be just short of the 200 mph mark.

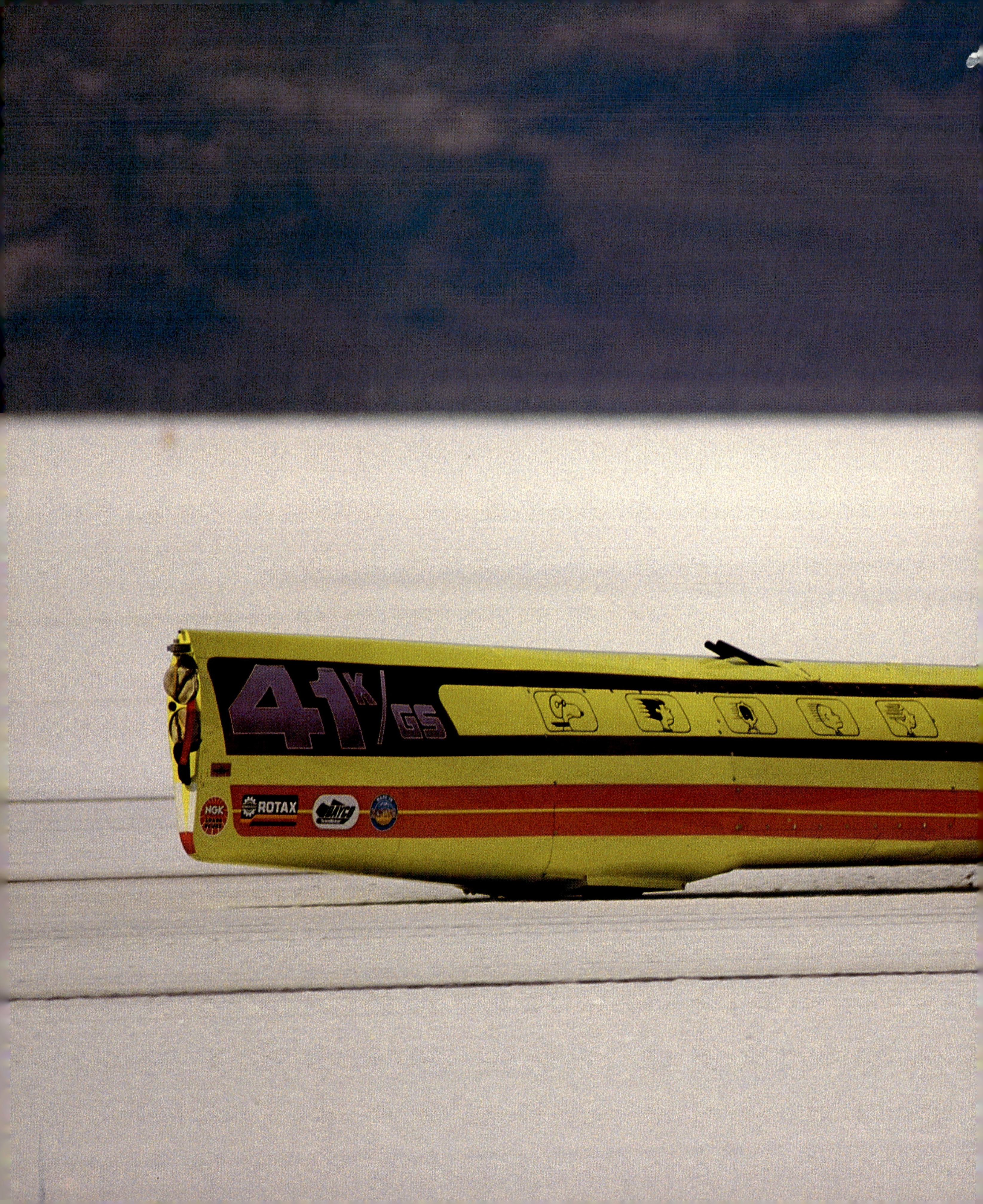
41K/GS
NGK
ROTAX

Charlie Brown, Snoopy and friends take a wild ride on the side of a K/Gas Streamliner powered by a 440 cc Rotax engine.

Vehicles on the salt

These examples are vehicles that are unique or represent a facet of the types of vehicles and teams that come to the salt each year. Some are high tech, others are from the old guard, and others are simply here to prove a point (speed) and probably won't appear on the salt again.

Longview Diesel
This truck has had many lives. It started out as a Navy fire truck in the military during World War II and continued with its fire duty after the war in a small community in Minnesota. The truck became a Bonneville racer in 1980 when it was fitted with a 2,000 hp, V-12, four turbo, Detroit Diesel engine. The *Buzzin Dozzen,* as it's called, runs in the modified diesel truck class and holds the existing class speed record of 178+ mph.

The driver, Bill Snyder, describes the run down the salt as working in a snowstorm, due to loose salt getting sucked into the cab and floating around. The two large skids on the front of the truck are to protect against a tire blowout or the loss of a rim. The Longview Diesel is a unique fixture each year as it roars down the salt trailing a long black cloud of smoke.

Racing Beat Mazda RX-7
The ultimate in high technology was achieved when a Mazda RX-7 driven by Don Sherman screamed down the salt in 1986 to set a class speed record of 238.442 mph. The car had a stock body, the same basic two-cylinder rotary engine that comes standard on an RX-7 and looked to all the world like your everyday sports car.

Beneath the almost-stock look (it sat pretty low and had smaller tires) was the high tech. The engine produced 530 hp from a mere 80 ci, thanks

The fastest diesel truck in the world, the Longview Diesel, smokes its way off the line. Weighing in at 12,480 lb., the monster takes all of 2,000 hp and a five-speed Allison gearbox to get up to speed. This truck, in exact configuration, is used in the truck drags and turns times in the high 12s with a terminal speed of 95 mph at the end of the quarter mile.

LONGVIEW DIESEL SERVICE INC
LONGVIEW DIESEL SERVICE
12V-71
INTERSTATE WOOD PRODUCTS

to twin turbos and an intercooling system filled with ice. The suspension wasn't your run of the road either. A racing suspension was fitted to help get the power to the salt and keep the car as low to the ground as possible.

The class record prior to driver Don Sherman's runs was 201.213 mph. One of the two-way runs for the record was 244.132 mph! To put this all into perspective one must realize that the record the little 80 ci Mazda broke was held by a V-8 with a displacement of 306 to 372 ci!

Lattin-Gillette *Red Head* streamliner

Jim Lattin and Elmo Gillette have campaigned the *Red Head* streamliner for seven years. During this time they set numerous records (three still stand) and placed six drivers in the prestigious 200 MPH Club. The car first raced at the salt in 1962 and set many records for the previous owners as well. The fastest the car has run is 330 mph with a blown Chrysler engine. Currently the car has aboard a 1949 Mercury engine displacing 274 ci with special Ardun heads attached. This placed the car into class XX/GS where it set a record of 212.040 mph.

The *Red Head* continues to prove its speedworthy design and recently helped add Jim Lattin's son Bill to the 200 MPH Club.

Kahler Porsche 911

Denny Kahler is one of the new racers at Bonneville Speed Week and represents a small three-member team effort that was successful the first time out.

The Kahler Porsche is a 1974 vintage 911S that has had the roof chopped and the rain gutters removed to lower the wind resistance. Also added was a new sloped front end for the same reason. The engine is 2000 cc with a turbocharger. Considering the modifications to the car and the engine type, the car was placed in E Modified Sports. The Porsche managed a top speed average of 183.737 mph to set a new class record.

Some support for the small teams comes from manufacturers that furnish shocks, tires and engine parts, but the majority of expenses are the owner's responsibility. Denny Kahler says he and his team will be back again next year to continue toward other speed records.

Banks Pontiac Firebird

What does it take to move a 5,000 pound car to record speeds? Lots of money, good engineering and a whole bunch of luck. With some help from Pontiac and a crew of superb engineers, Gale Banks has set some lofty records on the Bonneville salt. Imagine a stock-bodied Pontiac Firebird setting a record of 268.033 mph and hitting an official recorded speed of over 277 mph. This is the world's fastest passenger car!

Needless to say, stock bodied doesn't mean stock car. The Banks twin turbo, 454 ci engine turned out in excess of 1,600 hp with the help of a liquid intercooler. The suspension and drivetrain were re-engineered to help support the tremendous power of the engine, and Goodyear supplied special tires to get the power to the salt and make the speeds safer.

The Banks crew is not typical of the racers at Speed Week. They are the elemental group in crew size and resources. It might be said that Banks mounts an assault on the records. With a total of eighteen crew members having specialties in turbocharging, computers, wheels, tires and engines, their success is almost assured. Each goal attained has Gale Banks thinking up new ones. In sight is the Firebird attaining 300 mph.

Guthrie's motorcycles

Traveling all the way from Florida to run his motorcycles at speed down the salt, Scott Guthrie is what many people would call a "speed-o-holic." At the 1987 Speed Week competition he garnered no less than five new speed records. To accomplish this he had to qualify each bike; then at record runs he would be first in line with one of his bikes, make that run, leave that bike at mile seven, go back to the start line and make the record run with the next qualified bike. The same procedure would take place on the return runs for the record.

Currently Scott Guthrie holds eighteen different Speed Week motorcycle records.

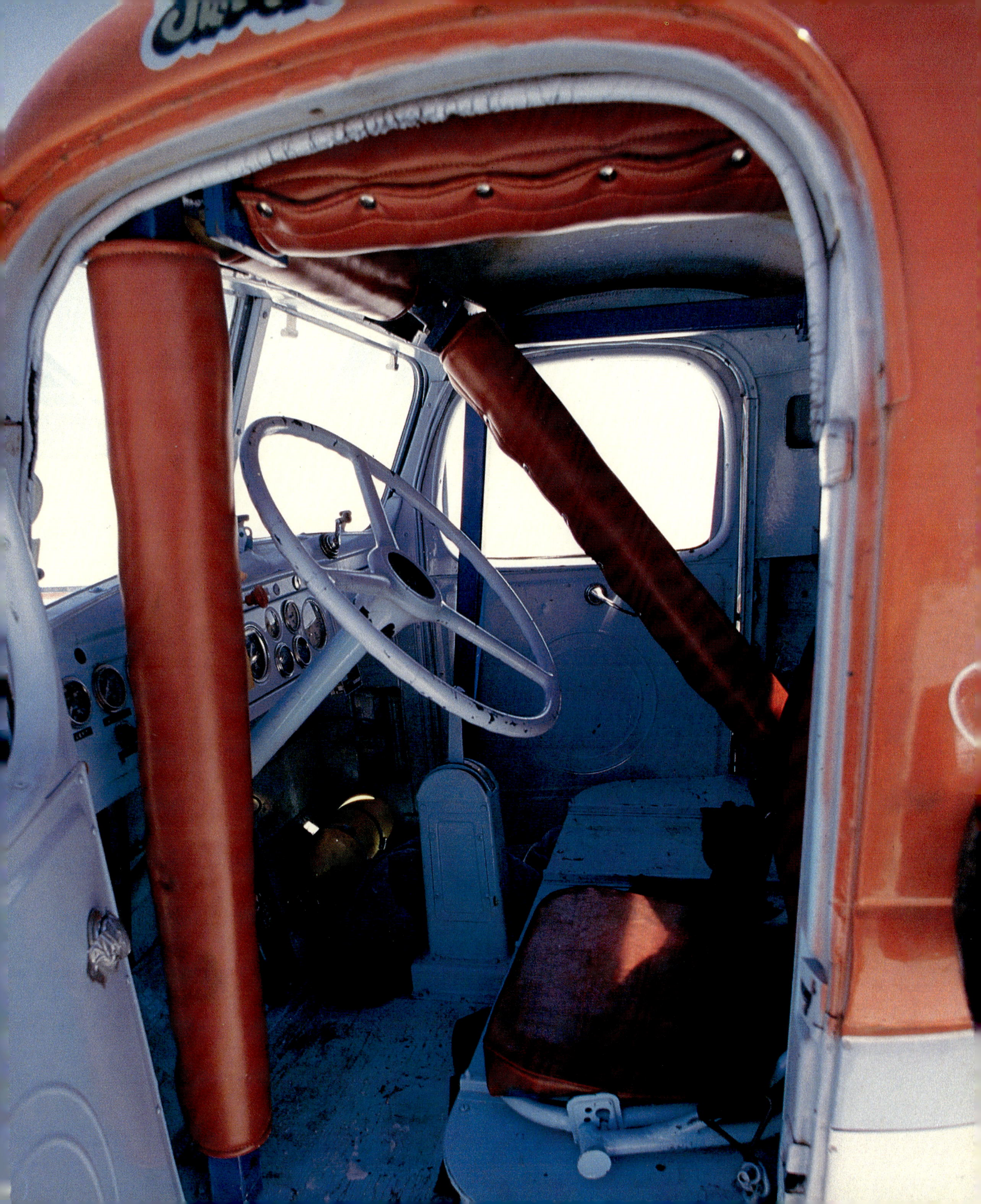

Previous page
The cockpit of a 172 mph racer. No racing Recaro seat, no electronic gauges or computers to monitor what's happening, just the bare basics of a forties-era fire truck. If the driver had time to look back during a run, all he'd see would be an impressive solid black wall of smoke that hangs in the air as the truck hastens down the white salt at a velocity uncommon to anything this size.

Six tires, twelve cylinders, four turbos, and 2,000 hp push this former fire truck to over 172.820 mph. The Detroit-Diesel-engine-powered truck has been smoking down the salt since 1980. The huge engine is good for only five runs down the salt before bearings wear out and cylinders seize due to the engine heat. The crew on this vehicle gets a lot of practice in rebuilding engines.

DOZZEN

The RX-7 sends up a cloud of salt as it runs the course at over 200 mph. Earlier in the week during a record attempt, driver Don Sherman lost traction on the moist salt and spun the rotary rocket at 200+ mph—a ride to match the best offered at any amusement park. The large amounts of power coupled with narrow tires make the need for smooth shifts imperative. The drive wheels can be spun loose on any shift with orbiting results.

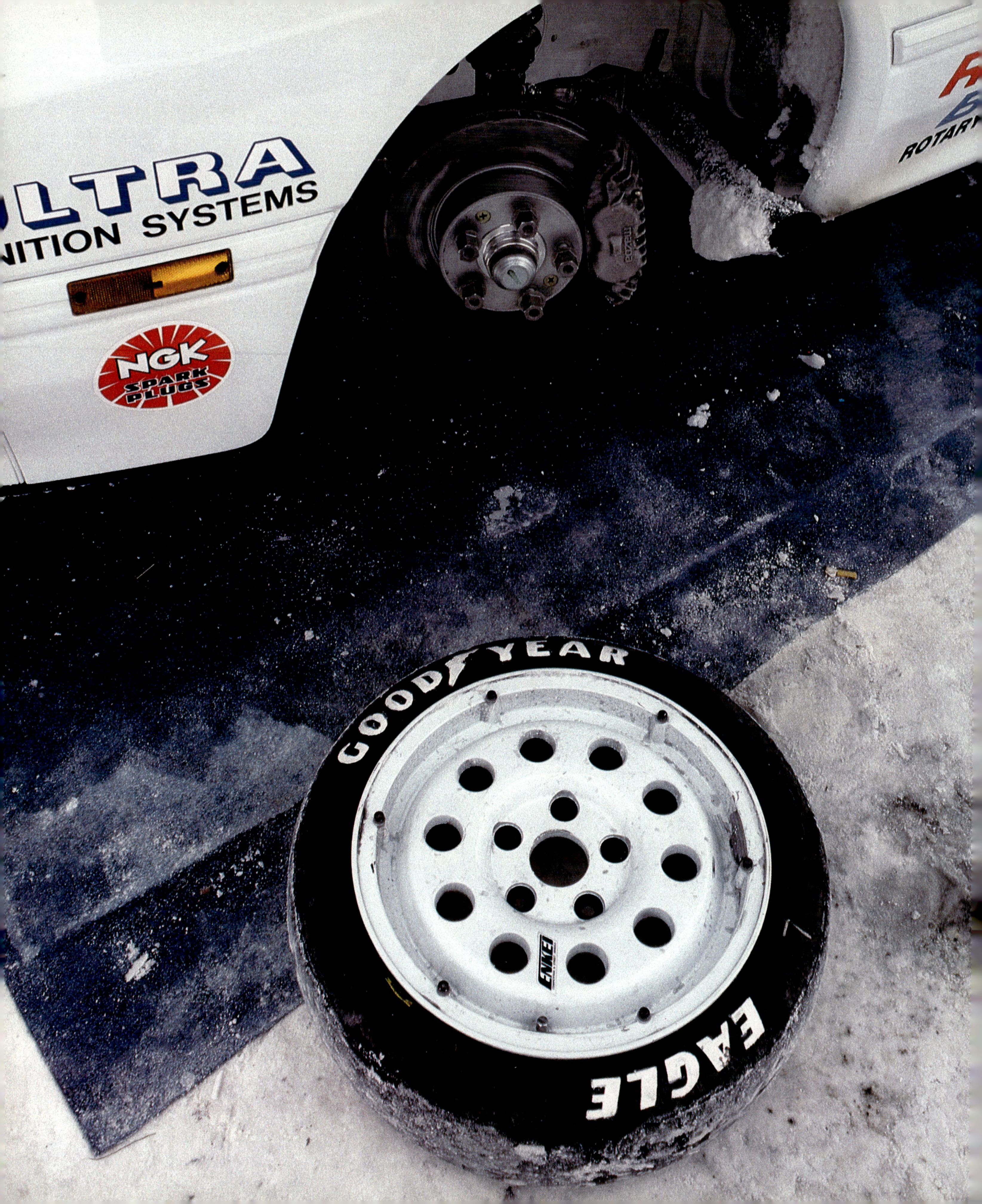

LTRA
NITION SYSTEMS
NGK
SPARK PLUGS
GOODYEAR
EAGLE

Special Goodyear tires and Enkei wheels helped the Mazda RX-7 Racing Beat effort. Since the car travels at over 200 mph, the tires needed are of a special variety designed for high speed. The rear tires are of a standard type used on the front of drag racing funny cars, while the RX-7's front tires were specially designed by Goodyear for the assault on the salt. Both traction and high-speed performance are factors in the tire design.

The engine compartment of the Rotary Rocket. The car puts out 530 hp from 80 ci by way of a two-rotor engine, twin turbos, a large ice-filled intercooler and a lot of expertise from the Racing Beat crew.

IGN
FUEL
TRANS
DIF
OIL TEMP
OIL PRESS
PRO-COMP II
MEMORY
PUSH TO ERASE
RPM
RECALL
WATER
BOOST PRESS
TRANS TEMP
mazda

The basic cockpit of the RX-7 is stock except for a complement of Auto Meter gauges to monitor the rotary engine's progress and a full roll cage to protect the driver. Monitoring gauges while trying to stay on course at over 200 mph is a difficult, but necessary, job for the drivers. Without the information from the previous run, it's impossible to make improvements on the car.

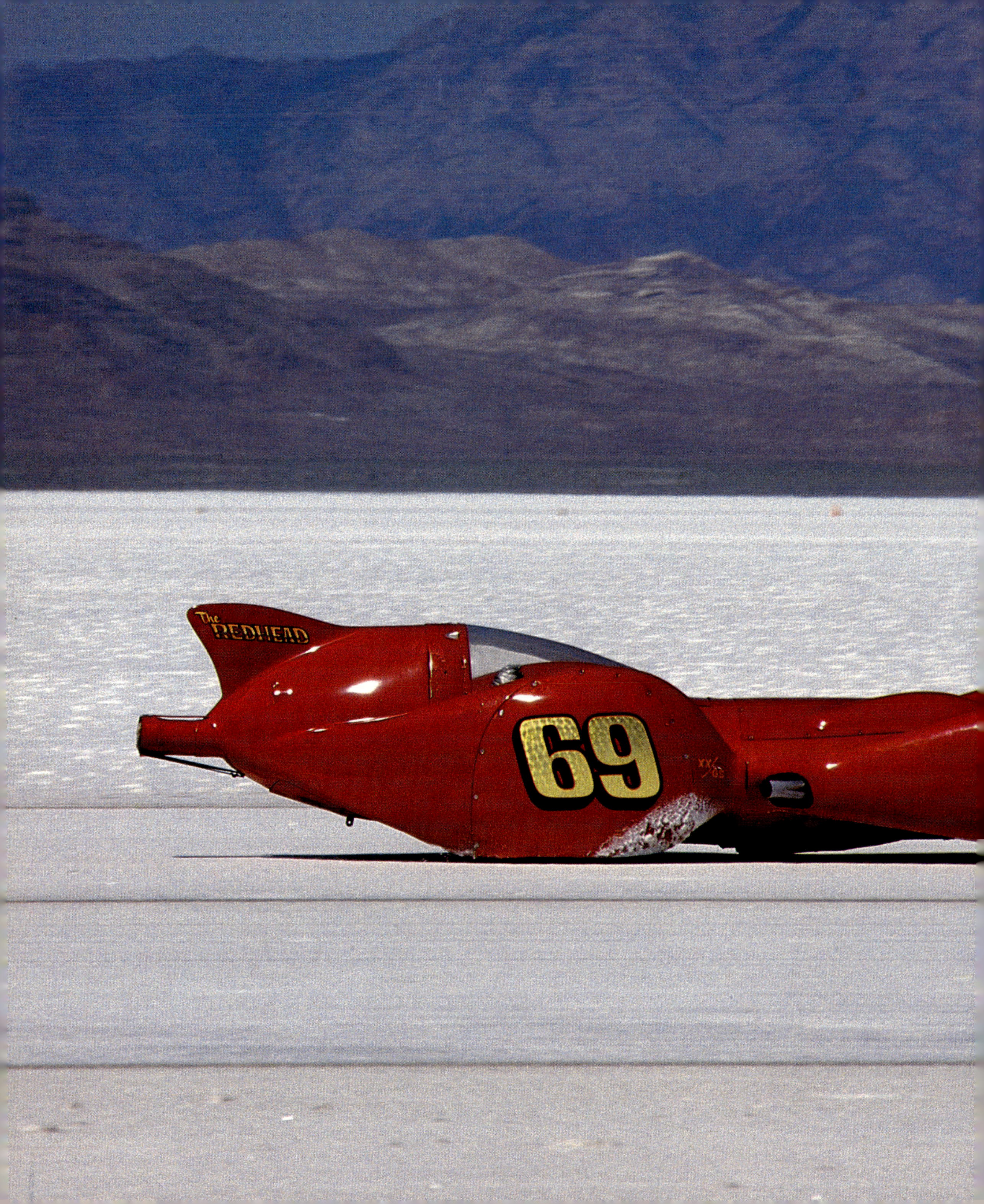
The
REDHEAD
69

The XX/Gas Streamliner Red Head, with Bill Lattin aboard, qualifying for a record of 212+ mph. Different engines can be placed in the same car so that it can qualify for other classes. The Red Head was timed at 330 mph with a blown Chrysler engine in 1965.

What is it like to take the sleek streamliner down the salt? Take a ride with Jim Lattin, one of the Red Head's owners and drivers, as he makes a run down the salt.

The car starts easily, but still needs a push to get it rolling because of the high gearing. With the engine rumbling its distinctive flathead sound, Jim waits till the engine temperature comes up and checks the oil pressure. When all looks right the canopy is fastened into place and the starting line official gives a thumbs-up to push down the empty track. Keeping an eye on the tach and slipping the clutch, the driver handles the shifts very gently to minimize wheel spin. The Red Head only has a two-speed transmission, so clutch slipping is necessary to keep up the revs.

Jim talks to himself as he gathers speed and the yellow markers start to flip by. He calls out the miles—at 200 mph things happen very quickly. Talking to the car, he maintains his position between the course's three lines and stays on the side of the center line that he believes is the smoothest. At over 200 mph in the timing traps, Jim must watch his tach to keep from pushing beyond the engine's capabilities. During record runs the car's engine must be in one piece to make a return run.

Counting markers, Jim sees mile five and starts the procedure for a clean shutdown: get off the gas, kick in the clutch and hit the electric switch to off. This routine keeps the plugs clean so it can be later determined if the engine ran lean or rich. It's all coasting from there. He pops the chute, and as soon as the car's down to 100 mph applies the brakes, then takes a slow turn to the right and off the course with a few minutes' wait for the crew to show up. It's not just a matter of putting the pedal to the metal and holding on.

The E/Modified 1974 Porsche of Denny Kahler with chute deployed. The red 911 has the top chopped, rain gutters removed, and a modified sloped nose to aid in streamlining. The turbocharged two-liter engine propelled the sleek Porsche to a class record of 183.737 mph. Kahler actually drives this speedster on the street, legally.

AUTOMOTION
KAHLER'S
EMS
Bosch
Authorized
Service
BOSCH
107
YOKOHAMA
VALVOLINE
KONI

The "long black lines" view of the Banks 1988 Pontiac Firebird Trans Am. This stock-looking Firebird can actually double the speed of its "stock" brothers that cruise America's streets. The Banks Firebird travels the distance of the race course (seven miles) in around one and a half minutes and at its top speed is covering 450 feet every second. After being push-started from the start line, driver Don Stringfellow takes the Firebird to 103 mph and 7112 rpm in first gear, all the while trying to minimize wheelspin; second gear sees the speed shoot up to 176 mph with a top engine rpm of 7548; third gear, 214 mph and still a problem of wheelspin at each shift; fourth at 263 mph at 7104 rpm; and, finally, fifth gear at a speed of over 270 mph as the car exits the speed traps. Not your everyday boulevard run.

Other features that set this Firebird apart from the street versions are an internal roll cage to protect the driver and a redesigned four-link suspension to alleviate the problem of getting the power to the salt. At the rear of the car where luggage might have gone is a 95-gallon intercooler tank to cool the intake air for the engine. The tank holds 250 lb. of crushed ice to supercool the air-fuel mixture prior to its entering the cylinders, giving optimum power.

Driver Don Stringfellow pilots the Banks Pontiac from a seat surrounded by gauges for monitoring the engine. The tachometer, oil pressure, fuel pressure, water pressure, manifold boost and the turbo's turbine inlet temperature gauges are all in the line of sight to help make the quick decisions needed to drive the car at speeds close to 300 mph.

Beside the seat are the shifter, levers to employ the braking chutes and two computers to monitor 32 analog, 16 digital and 6 rpm functions. The computers and an onboard video camera help to replay and evaluate the whole run later. The rest of the car's interior is relatively stock with the regular dash, tilt steering wheel and even the sound system, still intact.

115

The engine compartment of Gale Banks' car contains a V-8 454 ci big-block Pontiac engine with twin Garrett Indy turbos. A pair of Banks-Holley four-barrel carburetors funnel the pressurized fuel-air mixture to the cylinders. The engine has been further improved with special Banks pistons, a special grind crank and various Pontiac Motorsports parts. The end tally of total power is about 1,600 hp. This is one of the cleanest and tightest engine bays you'll ever see.

Scott Guthrie approaches the camera after a qualifying run. Scott has been known to qualify two bikes on the same day, only to have to shuttle back and forth the next morning to run both bikes the two ways required for a record. When Scott was asked how he felt on a speed run down the salt, his answer was "apprehensive." The reason for his concern is due to several factors that go beyond the problems associated with running cars for the record.

As cars run down the salt, they dig narrow trenches with their spinning wheels. Along comes a two-wheeled cycle at 200 mph and the tendency is for its wheels to follow the ruts. A motorcycle rider must pick his way down the course missing ruts, chuckholes and soft spots—at 200 mph! Another factor can be the wind, or the sudden lack of it. The rider leans against a side wind force, and if the wind suddenly stops, the bike veers into the direction the wind was coming from. If a rider loses it, he doesn't fall far, but the accompanying bike can cause bodily damage, as can the abrasive salt surface.

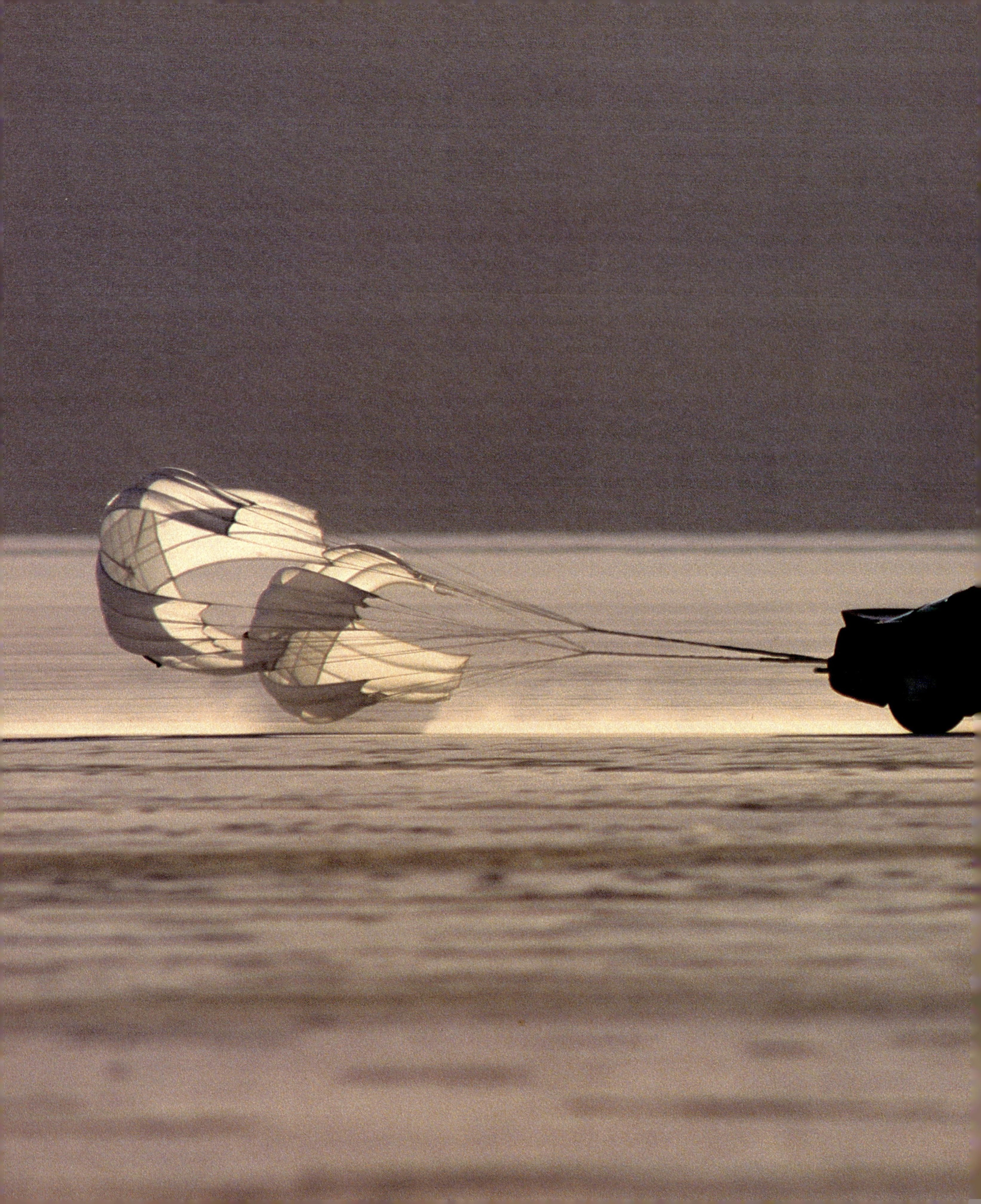

Stopping

The faster you go, the harder it is to stop. On vehicles that travel over 175 mph a drag chute is required to slow the racer, and on vehicles that exceed 300 mph two independent chutes are attached. There have been situations with a fast vehicle where the chutes were lost upon deployment and the vehicle has careened off the end of the course.

The Gale Banks Pontiac Firebird Trans Am with both chutes deployed at the end of a successful qualifying run of 265.553 mph. The chutes are so effective that the Pontiac doesn't have any brakes on the front wheels. The elimination of the front brakes helps in the streamlining of the car and saves on weight.

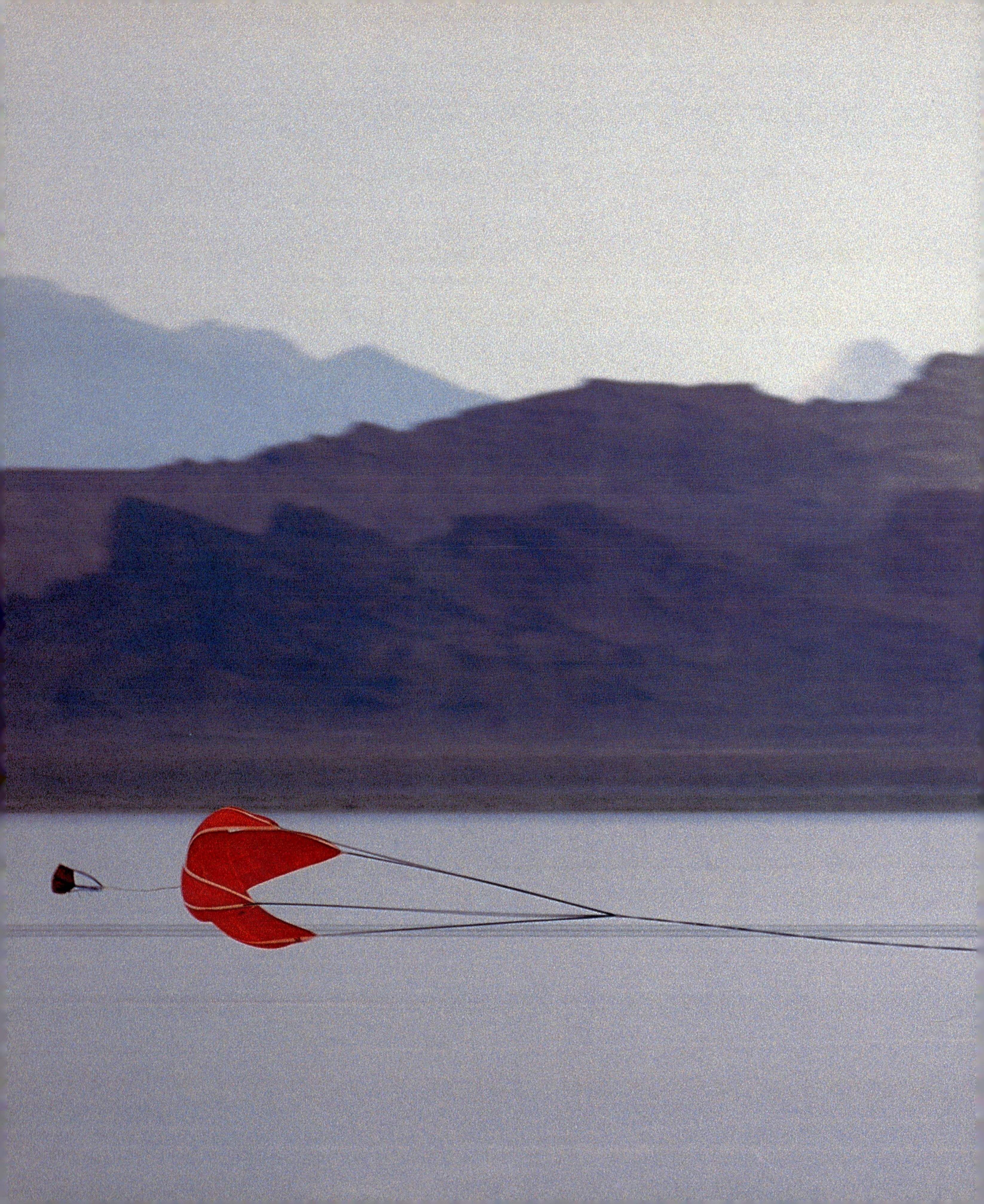

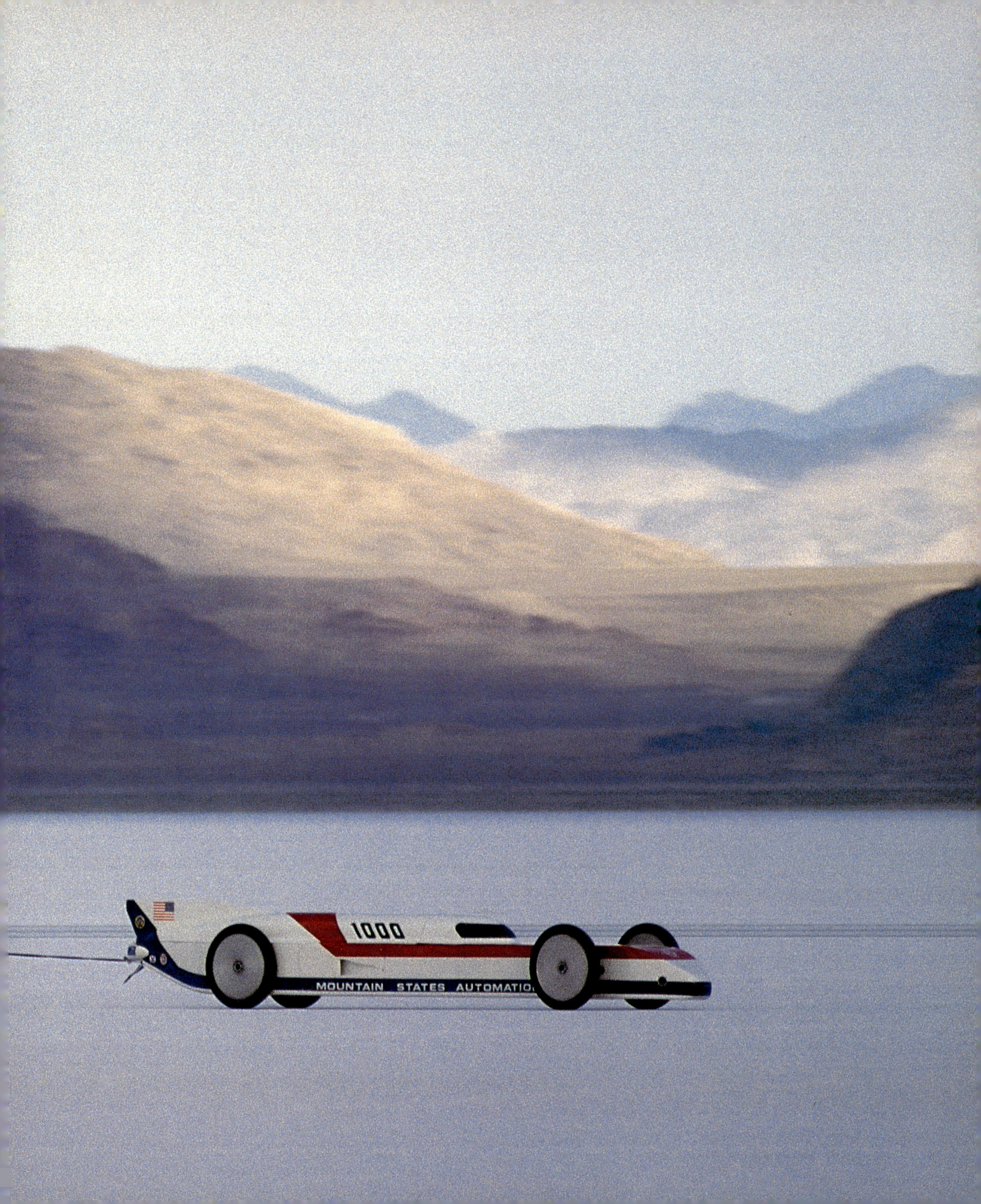
1000
MOUNTAIN STATES AUTOMATIO

Previous page
The J/Fuel Lakester is powered by a 748 cc Honda engine. It pops its chute at the end of a qualifying run of 145.625 mph. The smaller displacement classes of streamliners and lakesters are powered by motorcycle engines.

The driver steps out of the Goldenrod streamliner at the end of a qualifying run. This is one of the oldest cars still running on the salt, having run with numerous engine displacements since the late fifties.

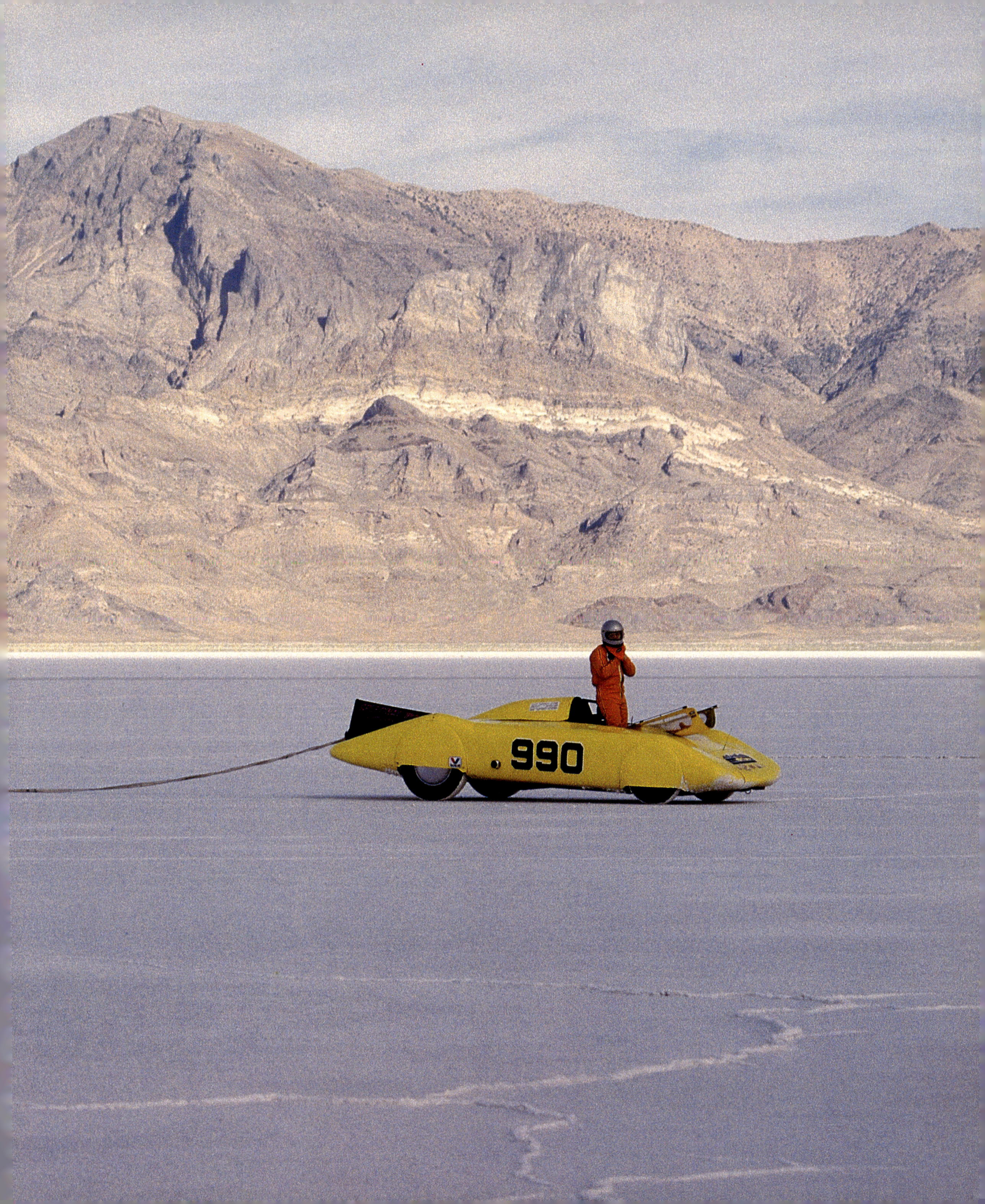
990

Check the engine and pack the chute while you wait for the chase crew to bring you the results of your run and then slowly tow you back to the pits. Car number 216 is a competition coupe capable of over 200 mph.

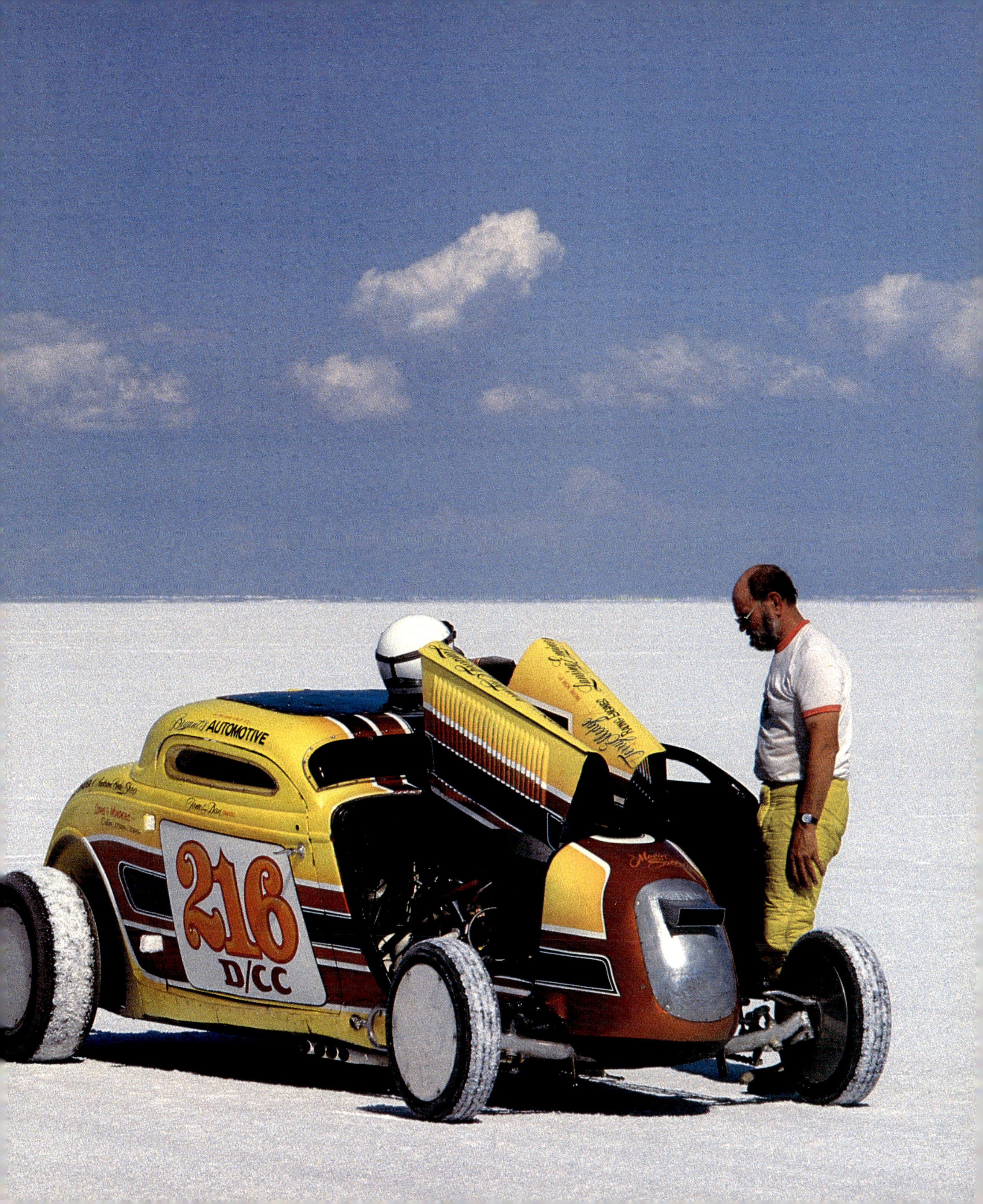
AUTOMOTIVE
216
D/CC

The 200 MPH Club

Drivers of cars and motorcycles that exceed 200 mph in the breaking of a record are recognized by being inducted into the 200 MPH Club. Note that a record must be broken to qualify. Just going 200 mph is not enough.

The club is fairly exclusive, with only a few drivers making the requirements each year. Since 1937, 206 men and four women have qualified for membership.

Driver Don Sherman displays the hat that signifies his accomplishment of breaking a speed record at over 200 mph. Don accomplished the feat in the Mazda RX-7 that went 238.442 mph. Since 1937 only 206 men and four women have earned entry into the prestigious 200 MPH Club. Even though many dragsters set records at over 200 mph, the significant difference is that the record must be a sanctioned two-way run.

Each year the car owners and their crews return to the salt for the same reason: to go ever faster and meet with old friends who have similar aspirations of speed. There seems also to be a resurgence of Speed Week in the number of new participants. The reason may be that drag strips around the country are closing and the hot rod talent is coming to the salt.

May the salt be dry, the thunderstorms wait, and the thrill of full throttle down the long black line continue to be with them.